CONFLICT *to* HARMONY

THE COUPLE'S GUIDE TO END MONEY CONFLICTS AND ACHIEVE FINANCIAL COMPATIBILITY

CHAE WAUGH

Paperback ISBN: 979-8-9991815-6-5

Hardcover ISBN: 979-8-9991815-1-0

eBook ISBN: 979-8-9991815-7-2

Contributions by: Maricela Waugh

Edited by: Live Your Dreams Out Loud Publishing

Cover design by: Live Your Dreams Out Loud Publishing

Printed in the United States of America

The Spicy Life Inc.

352 Topanga Canyon Blvd. #204

Canoga Park, CA 91304-2344

www.thespicylife.com

To my beautiful and talented wife, our partnership serves as the motivation to assist others on their path.

CONTENTS

INTRODUCTION

The dynamics between partners in a relationship have been the focus of many studies that look to explain the age-old question: What makes us compatible? Compatibility is to relationships what a key is to a lock—the right fit opens the door to everything the relationship has to offer. When we explore the dynamics of relationships, we often look to what characteristics, traits, likes, and dislikes we have in common to help us form a bond. Do we like the same music or foods, or do we enjoy doing similar things or hobbies, like traveling? Couples long for the things that make our connections that much more meaningful and, hopefully, long-lasting.

While what brings us together is super important, it's what breaks us apart that puts our relationship to the test. Conflict is almost certainly unavoidable, and compatibility often isn't enough to overcome the potential fallout that conflict brings. We know that there are several reasons why conflict occurs in a relationship, but the one topic we're here to about is finances. A study published in the *Journal of Family Issues* revealed that in 40 percent of conflicts reported by individuals in long-term relationships, finances were the main reason. (2) That's a significant amount of conflict attributed to finances. It would seem that we can connect on so many levels, but the one level we seem to not be able to connect on as effectively is finances. We can also pinpoint what specific aspects of finances and money management usually triggers conflict. But with all issues, the real value isn't in just analyzing the problem after the conflict, but in identifying the reasons for potential issues before the conflict occurs.

So, how do we accomplish this? We could all adopt the approach of talking about our finances before we get into a long-term commitment. However, we know for certain that couples typically avoid talking about money in the early stages of their relationship. The last thing anyone wants to talk about while dating is finances. Finances are so off-limits that they rank lower than the ex as far as topics to discuss while dating. "The Spicy Life" surveyed 100 clients, and 82 percent said that, while dating, they would rather talk about a previous relationship or an ex-partner than talk about finances. (3) We don't like to talk about finances, yet finances control so much of our lives and our relationships. Finances can either bring couples closer or drive them apart—often the latter. Money has played a role in the collapse of empires, nations, and countless marriages. In fact, it remains one of the leading causes of divorce. (4)

In my book, *Marriage & Finances*, I explore this problem from the perspective of increasing financial literacy. I also introduce in the first chapter the concept of financial compatibility, where I offer an assessment known formally as the Financial Compatibility Assessment (FCA) for partners to use to engage with each other and discover more about their relationship with money from childhood to adulthood. They can use the results to discuss areas of similarities and differences. While encouraging couples to engage in a constructive conversation about finances is important, research indicates that individuals respond better to more structured guidance and frameworks when it comes to identifying and solving a problem.

I developed the FCA as a framework to identify topics that could cause conflicts in relationships. The FCA is a quantifiable and measurable approach to discovering how financially compatible you are with your partner and what you need to work on to really be fully aligned with each other financially. "Understanding each other's relationship with finances is as important as discussing common interests or hobbies. It's a significant factor in determining compatibility and plays a huge role in the dynamics of the relationship." (3) While I included the assessment in the book, I did not include a full breakdown of the 41-topic survey that touched on childhood experiences and adulthood behavior. Now, for the first time, I am unlocking the research behind the FCA and the reason why those 41 topics are essential to gaining a full understanding of how compatible you are with your partner. I have included updated and more relevant data to improve upon the research conducted nearly three years ago.

You will have the opportunity to take the assessment along with your partner. After you take the FCA, you will have a chance to explore each of the assessment topics and evaluate your responses. I've dedicated a chapter for each topic that explores why the topic matters, as well as some key discussion points to talk through with your partner. This book will provide you with a full perspective of what it means to be financially compatible and provide you with a clear roadmap to get you from incompatible to full alignment. You and your partner will first take the FCA and calculate your scores. You will then take a deep dive into why each question matters and engage in key discussion topics with each other. We will dive into all aspects of personal finances, and along the way, we will break down and hopefully highlight some common misconceptions and limiting beliefs about finances and the role they play in the dynamics of your relationship. In the end, you will create a Financial Compatibility Action Plan to serve as your roadmap to a more harmonious financial journey with your partner.

Let's begin this journey with a pledge. I want you to turn and look at your partner and repeat the following pledge:

> *"I pledge to keep an open mind and an open heart. I pledge to listen to your perspective and embrace it, even if it is different from mine. I pledge to be willing to accept a new shared perspective in order to improve our finances and relationship."*

Before you and your partner take the FCA, let's learn a little more about it and explore its many benefits. Yes, I am a firm believer in learning the science of things in order to get to a higher level of understanding. Besides, I did a considerable amount of research to get us here, so it's only right that I get to share that work with you in the hopes that you will not only understand but appreciate the method that I firmly believe will enable you to be financially compatible with your partner. Don't worry; the book isn't all about research and analysis. This book is an interactive experience as you explore the topics and engage with each other, mixed in with a few references from some brilliant people, to empower you to enrich your commitment to each other and your financial well-being.

THE FINANCIAL COMPATIBILITY ASSESSMENT

The idea of financial compatibility has been around for some time, and it has been studied extensively. So, what is financial compatibility? In an article by Theresa E. DiDonato Ph.D. in the *Psychology Today*, she states that financial compatibility is not about making the same amount of money or coming from the same amount of money. It's about people's approach to money (5). She goes on to say that you can gauge your financial compatibility by thinking about how you and your partner navigate major money decisions. Financial incompatibility predicts relationship instability, and when it comes to marriage, it is a predictive indicator for divorce (5). The connection between financial compatibility and the health of your relationship is undeniable. So how do we move toward becoming more financially compatible with our partners?

FINANCIAL INTIMACY IS NOT OPTIONAL, IT'S REQUIRED

Before we can begin to uncover the drivers of financial compatibility, we first have to unlock the benefits of financial intimacy. Financial intimacy involves gaining an understanding of each other's approach to personal finances. In order to do that, we need to achieve a level of financial intimacy. The concept of financial intimacy is explored in my book *Marriage & Finances*. "Financial intimacy refers to the level of openness and communication between couples regarding their finances. It involves sharing financial information, discussing financial goals, and making joint decisions about money matters. Financial intimacy is vital to a healthy relationship, as it fosters trust, transparency, and a shared sense of responsibility for your financial well-being." (3)

Financial intimacy between partners opens up the possibilities of understanding the true nature of why finical conflict exists and what can be done to avoid it. Hence, it would be helpful to have access to a tool to promote financial intimacy as a means to examine compatibility and avoid conflict. This was the driving force behind the creation of the financial compatibility assessment (FCA).

THE FCA INCLUDES TOPICS MEANT TO EVALUATE COMPATIBILITY

The Financial Compatibility Assessment (FCA) was created with the purpose of truly understanding the multifaceted nature of money as a driving force behind conflict in relationships. The FCA seeks to provide clarity on the cause of conflict by identifying the differences in your experience with money and finances growing up, as well the differences in your current beliefs about money and finances. To accomplish this, we researched 152 topics on money and finances that play an influential role in driving conflict between partners. The topics covered a wide range of issues from childhood experiences with finances to how that person now approaches money as an adult. Through our research, we found that for the most part, individuals who observed and were taught good money management habits as a child continued those habits as an adult. We found that most people acknowledged the need for good money management regardless if they practiced good money management or not. Lastly, we found that most individuals acknowledged the need to teach their children good money management habits, but there wasn't a broad consensus on how.

FINANCIAL COMPATIBILITY IS THE SUM OF THREE PARTS

The research also found that not all of the 152 topics had a significant impact on driving compatibility. Out of the 152 topics included in the survey, there were **41 key topics** that we found to be the most likely to cause conflict and therefore more likely to impact compatibility. These 41 topics make up the Financial Compatibility Assessment. Three unique themes emerged that defined each of the 41 topics.

1. ***Your experiences with money and finances growing up.***
2. ***Your current practices and beliefs about money and finances.***
3. ***How you plan to teach your children about money and finances.***

Each of these themes represents an intersection of your experiences with money and finances with your partner's experiences with money and finances. The resulting number of questions across each component is a direct indication of the significance each theme has on predicting conflict and driving compatibility.

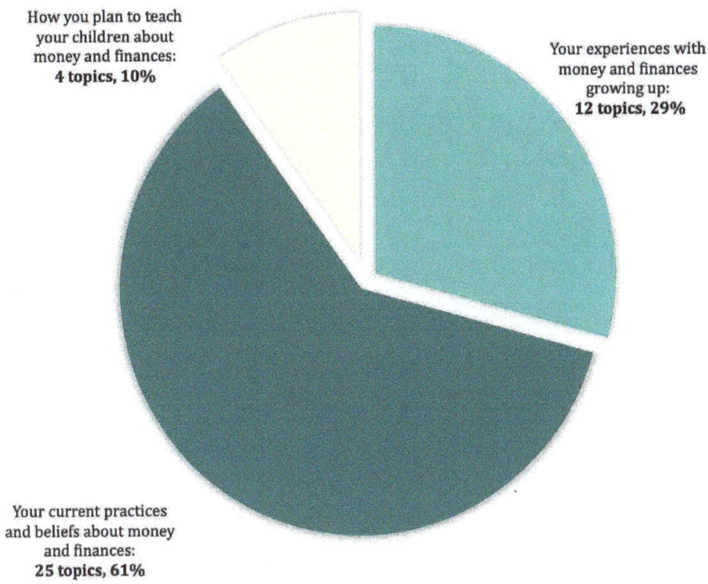

Your experiences with money and finances growing up

The first theme of financial compatibility has to do with the similarities and differences between your experience and your partner's experience with money and finances growing up and the influence your parents may have had on those experiences. This theme represents 12 topics, or 29 percent of the FCA. Shared experiences do not necessarily translate into financial compatibility as it's only one piece, albeit an important one, of the puzzle. Your younger years were very formidable, and during that time, the influence of your parent's financial habits often formed the basis for your financial habits as an adult.

Your experiences could lead you to have a positive outlook on money and finances, or conversely, your experiences could be the catalyst for limiting beliefs about money and finances. When developing the financial compatibility assessment, we included a number of topics that studies show have a significant impact on how we view and approach money and finances. These topics include how your parents approached spending, saving, and budgeting, as well as what they may have taught you about money and finances growing up.

Your current practices and beliefs about money and finances

The largest theme of financial compatibility has to do with your current practice and behavior when it comes to money and finances compared to those of your partner. This theme represents 25 topics, or 61 percent of the FCA, about things like how you use credit cards to your views on spending and saving and what financial information you disclose to your partner. Research shows this theme is the most important factor in compatibility, offering the greatest opportunity for you and your partner to make meaningful changes in how you approach finances—helping shift your relationship from conflict to harmony. Although this is the most significant aspect of compatibility, your current approach relies on your experiences to provide a bigger picture of your relationship with money compared with your partner's.

How you plan to teach your children about money and finances

The last piece of the puzzle, when it comes to compatibility, has to do with your intended approach to educating your children about money and finances compared to your partner's. This theme represents four topics, or 10 percent of the FCA. Studies show that this component does not play as much of a role in driving compatibility compared with your experiences and current approach. However, it still plays a role in driving conflict down the road. Prospective parents tend not to disagree on these types of matters when discussing plans for starting a family. This is because the topic of how they plan to teach their children good financial habits is the last topic of conversation, if it even comes at all.

So, you never really know if you and your partner have a similar mindset around teaching your kids about money until the time comes to teach your kids about money. The FCA includes topics targeted at understanding your views on specific aspects of money and finances related to children against the views of your partner. The goal is to understand and reconcile those views now to avoid conflict down the road.

THE FCA IS A VEHICLE FOR TRANSPARENCY

The Financial Compatibility Assessment is an effective tool to facilitate the discovery of each partner's financial situation and the experiences of both individuals in relation to money management. The ultimate outcome is to not only help get a better understanding of each partner's approach and attitude toward money, but also to discover any areas of potential conflict and determine a way to move forward on a path of compatibility through transparency and adaptability.

Both partners complete the assessment separately, as this ensures that they are both able to give an honest account of their financial attitudes without the influence of the other. Honesty is extremely important in order to facilitate the level of transparency needed to achieve a full understanding of each partner's approach and attitude toward money. The comparison of their responses serves as a basis for further discussion, focusing on the contrasts and similarities of their money management habits and financial values.

This level of transparency will reveal points of conflict and situations that will require a level of adaptability to transform financial conflict into financial harmony. It is expected that you may find that you have differing views on some aspects of money management, and this will require both partners to compromise and adjust their views. Adaptability enables people in a relationship to transform differences into opportunities for development and teamwork.

Adaptability is also an important factor as it will enable couples to come up with a financial plan that meets each of their needs while being in harmony with the set goals they create together. Financial compatibility isn't about one person's approach prevailing over the other's; it's about blending their strengths and finding a balance that works for both.

THE FCA PROVIDES A NUMBER OF BENEFITS

Through the FCA, it is possible to understand how your past experiences affect the financial decisions you make in the present. The FCA is especially useful in creating a safe forum through which couples can discuss personal finance topics since such topics are often sensitive and may be challenging to discuss. The FCA allows for the understanding of each partner's values and the values each partner has in common. This approach is effective as it empowers couples to develop a combined financial plan that considers both perspectives. This approach is also healthier as it has been proven to have a far more significant impact on the well-being of the relationship. The FCA has several advantages that can help improve a couple's relationship by helping the couple gain better insight into each other's financial values and habits.

Identification of potential conflicts

From this point, the FCA helps to determine the areas that may cause conflict based on the financial views of each partner. As you begin to review your results, you will identify areas you have in common and, more importantly, areas where you have differing perspectives. These areas where you have a different *experience*, *approach*, and *sentiment* tend to cause conflict.

Experience relates to topics that you've dealt with in the past, such as childhood events. Experiences cannot be changed; however, you may find that conflicts arise because of differences in your experiences versus the bond that can come from shared experiences.

Approach relates to the manner in which you deal with a topic, such as your approach to taking on debt or if you use a budget or not. You can take a different approach, but we see conflict arise from partners who take different approaches to a number of topics on money management.

Sentiment refers to your attitude or stance on a topic that you may not have experienced yet, such as your stance on joint accounts prior to getting married, or your stance on paying for your child's education, provided you don't already have children who are in college. Sentiments can also change. We find that conflicts do arise from partners who have differing sentiments on a variety of topics.

These are the areas that will likely be the cause of conflict if they aren't already. By identifying the potential conflict areas, you can take a more proactive approach to resolving the potential conflicts before they come up and a more active approach to conflict resolution if the issues have already surfaced.

Improved communication

The FCA facilitates open and honest conversations about your finances with your partner, a topic that can often be uncomfortable or challenging for couples. "Talking about money can be a delicate matter leading to disagreements or strained relationships." (3) The FCA provides a structured avenue to discuss your finances and emphasizes the importance of using effective communication methods in order to work through differences. The saying "practice makes perfect" comes to mind as you navigate difficult conversations and become better at communicating with your partner, helping to build a stronger, more transparent relationship.

Alignment of financial goals

The assessment will help to start a discussion about your financial priorities and goals; thus, it can help you and your partner get on the same page about what you want to achieve. "Your financial priorities and goals directly reflect your values and beliefs regarding money, allowing your partner to understand your values and see if your values align with theirs." (3) This is especially important for any couple who wants to work toward common financial goals in the long run.

"Establishing financial goals and tracking progress can help you stay accountable to your financial commitments." (3) Through the FCA, you will have the opportunity to reevaluate your financial goals to ensure that you and your partner are in full alignment to help avoid conflicts down the road.

Increased understanding

As you discuss your assessment results with your partner, you will learn quite a bit about each other. You will look into each partner's financial history as well as their current financial situation to come up with a sound conclusion as to why they act the way they do with money. Building understanding through empathy is essential for resolving conflicts and creating a plan that helps your relationship thrive. When you approach each other with empathy, it becomes easier to take accountability for any past financial habits that may have contributed to tension. Accountability is absolutely necessary in order to develop a financial compatibility action plan to help create a more harmonious relationship.

Improved financial planning

The FCA will provide some key ingredients needed to develop and execute an effective financial plan. Not only will you gain the perspective needed to meet each other's needs, but you will also understand what you will need to incorporate to avoid conflicts down the road. Your financial planning will be a whole lot easier as you understand each other's way of managing money, as well as their financial objectives. You will perform financial planning around areas like budgeting, saving, and investing in a way that is acceptable to both partners.

Strengthened relationship

The ultimate goal of the FCA is to improve your relationship and even take it to the next level. You and your partner need to discuss financial issues in order to reduce conflict and develop trust through transparency, understanding, and, most importantly, teamwork. This will enhance the relationship, supporting the idea that working together to gain financial harmony can, in fact, strengthen the bond between you and your partner and make the partnership more stable and able to overcome any outside pressures. Engaging in the FCA process empowers you and your partner to take an active role in managing your finances, which will boost your confidence in financial decision-making and improve the overall health of your relationship.

TAKE THE FINANCIAL COMPATIBILITY ASSESSMENT

The following pages have two identical assessments, one for each partner. Each partner will provide a response to the topic by selecting true or false and placing a checkmark in the appropriate box. Each partner should complete the assessment separately and avoid looking at each other's responses until it's time to review the assessment. Approach each topic truthfully and to the best of your knowledge, as some of the topics will be about your childhood and your recollections of how your parents handled finances.

Partner 1 (P1) Initials: ____________	**T**	**F**
1. My parents taught me about managing money.	✓	
2. My parents were careful about taking on debt.		✓

Once you have completed the assessment, proceed to the next page to calculate your results. There, you will find the assessment answer key. The True (T) and False (F) columns include a score of 1 or 0, which is the ideal response for each topic. Enter a **1** or **0** that corresponds to your response for each topic. To determine your score, add the total for columns **P1** and record your scores in the **Total** row. Repeat this process for Partner two (**P2**).

P1: __________ **P2:** __________	**T**	**F**	**P1**	**P2**
1. My parents taught me about managing money.	1	0	1	
2. My parents were careful about taking on debt.	1	0	0	

Partner 1 (P1) Initials: ________

		T	F
1.	My parents taught me about managing money.		
2.	My parents were careful about taking on debt.		
3.	My parents had frequent disagreements over how to spend money.		
4.	My parents emphasized the need to save for emergencies.		
5.	I grew up in a dual-income household.		
6.	My parents set goals for the things they needed to purchase.		
7.	My parents often faced financial difficulties.		
8.	My parents created a budget to live on and followed it.		
9.	My parents shopped around for the best deal before making a purchase.		
10.	My parents were cautious about using credit cards.		
11.	My parents used coupons.		
12.	My parents paid the bills on time.		
13.	I have a budget and live within it.		
14.	I use coupons.		

Partner 1 (P1) Initials: ________

#	Statement	T	F
15.	I pay my bills on time each month.		
16.	I balance my checkbook every month.		
17.	I set goals for the things I want to purchase.		
18.	When choosing an item to buy, I should select the most expensive option if I can afford it.		
19.	I pay my entire credit card statement balances each month.		
20.	Credit cards are for emergencies only.		
21.	A credit card can be a valuable tool to improve your finances.		
22.	I would take on more debt than planned to buy my forever home.		
23.	I should control the money in the marriage.		
24.	I believe it is important to save.		
25.	I should be able to put money away and not tell my partner.		
26.	I would never consider opening a joint account.		
27.	I would not like it if my partner made more money than me.		

Partner 1 (P1) Initials: ________

	Statement	T	F
28.	I should be able to lend money to a relative without first speaking with my partner.		
29.	I can make large purchases without consulting my partner.		
30.	It is okay for my partner to question how I spend money.		
31.	I am comfortable disclosing my income before marriage.		
32.	I am comfortable disclosing my debts before marriage.		
33.	I am comfortable disclosing my credit score before marriage.		
34.	My knowledge of finances is limited, and I would prefer my partner to handle it.		
35.	I would always be honest with my partner about how I spend money.		
36.	I set aside a portion of each paycheck to go toward savings.		
37.	I make contributions to a retirement account.		
38.	Children should learn the value of money.		
39.	I plan to share my financial situation with my children.		
40.	Children should be given the chance to manage their own money.		

Partner 1 (P1) Initials: ________

	T	F
41. My children should pay for their own college education.		

Partner 2 (P2) Initials: ________

		T	F
1.	My parents taught me about managing money.		
2.	My parents were careful about taking on debt.		
3.	My parents had frequent disagreements over how to spend money.		
4.	My parents emphasized the need to save for emergencies.		
5.	I grew up in a dual-income household.		
6.	My parents set goals for the things they needed to purchase.		
7.	My parents often faced financial difficulties.		
8.	My parents created a budget to live on and followed it.		
9.	My parents shopped around for the best deal before making a purchase.		
10.	My parents were cautious about using credit cards.		
11.	My parents used coupons.		
12.	My parents paid the bills on time.		
13.	I have a budget and live within it.		
14.	I use coupons.		

Partner 2 (P2) Initials: ________

	Statement	T	F
15.	I pay my bills on time each month.		
16.	I balance my checkbook every month.		
17.	I set goals for the things I want to purchase.		
18.	When choosing an item to buy, I should select the most expensive option if I can afford it.		
19.	I pay my entire credit card statement balances each month.		
20.	Credit cards are for emergencies only.		
21.	A credit card can be a valuable tool to improve your finances.		
22.	I would take on more debt than planned to buy my forever home.		
23.	I should control the money in the marriage.		
24.	I believe it is important to save.		
25.	I should be able to put money away and not tell my partner.		
26.	I would never consider opening a joint account.		
27.	I would not like it if my partner made more money than me.		

Partner 2 (P2) Initials: ________	**T**	**F**
28. I should be able to lend money to a relative without first speaking with my partner.		
29. I can make large purchases without consulting my partner.		
30. It is okay for my partner to question how I spend money.		
31. I am comfortable disclosing my income before marriage.		
32. I am comfortable disclosing my debts before marriage.		
33. I am comfortable disclosing my credit score before marriage.		
34. My knowledge of finances is limited, and I would prefer my partner to handle it.		
35. I would always be honest with my partner about how I spend money.		
36. I set aside a portion of each paycheck to go toward savings.		
37. I make contributions to a retirement account.		
38. Children should learn the value of money.		
39. I plan to share my financial situation with my children.		
40. Children should be given the chance to manage their own money.		

Partner 2 (P2) Initials: ________

	T	F
41. My children should pay for their own college education.		

P1: _______ P2: _______	T	F	P1	P2
1. My parents taught me about managing money.	1	0		
2. My parents were careful about taking on debt.	1	0		
3. My parents had frequent disagreements over how to spend money.	0	1		
4. My parents emphasized the need to save for emergencies.	1	0		
5. I grew up in a dual-income household.	1	0		
6. My parents set goals for the things they needed to purchase.	1	0		
7. My parents often faced financial difficulties.	0	1		
8. My parents created a budget to live on and followed it.	1	0		
9. My parents shopped around for the best deal before making a purchase.	1	0		
10. My parents were cautious about using credit cards.	1	0		
11. My parents used coupons.	1	0		
12. My parents paid the bills on time.	1	0		
13. I have a budget and live within it.	1	0		

P1:_______ P2:_______	T	F	P1	P2
14. I use coupons.	1	0		
15. I pay my bills on time each month.	1	0		
16. I balance my checkbook every month.	1	0		
17. I set goals for the things I want to purchase.	1	0		
18. When choosing an item to buy, I should select the most expensive option if I can afford it.	0	1		
19. I pay my entire credit card statement balances each month.	1	0		
20. Credit cards are for emergencies only.	0	1		
21. A credit card can be a valuable tool to improve your finances.	1	0		
22. I would take on more debt than planned to buy my forever home.	0	1		
23. I should control the money in the marriage.	0	1		
24. I believe it is important to save.	1	0		
25. I should be able to put money away and not tell my partner.	0	1		

P1: _______ P2: _______	T	F	P1	P2
26. I would never consider opening a joint account.	0	1		
27. I would not like it if my partner made more money than me.	0	1		
28. I should be able to lend money to a relative without first speaking with my partner.	0	1		
29. I can make large purchases without consulting my partner.	0	1		
30. It is okay for my partner to question how I spend money.	1	0		
31. I am comfortable disclosing my income before marriage.	1	0		
32. I am comfortable disclosing my debts before marriage.	1	0		
33. I am comfortable disclosing my credit score before marriage.	1	0		
34. My knowledge of finances is limited, and I would prefer my partner to handle it.	0	1		
35. I would always be honest with my partner about how I spend money.	1	0		

P1: ______ P2: ______	T	F	P1	P2
36. I set aside a portion of each paycheck to go toward savings.	1	0		
37. I make contributions to a retirement account.	1	0		
38. Children should learn the value of money.	1	0		
39. I plan to share my financial situation with my children.	1	0		
40. Children should be given the chance to manage their own money.	1	0		
41. My children should pay for their own college education.	0	1		
		Total		

YOUR FINANCIAL COMPATIBILITY MATRIX

The results of your FCA are not just about the total score. Your total score simply gives you a comparison against the ideal response to each topic. This is the baseline, which is a score of 41. Your score is a culmination of all three components of the FCA and how you compare to the baseline. The further away you are from the baseline indicates where there could be areas of concern regarding your personal relationship with money and finances. So, if you scored a 41, a perfect score, it means you most likely have great money management skills and a good credit score to boot. But that doesn't mean you won't have conflicts with your partner. As a matter of fact, I would wager that this person with a perfect score would have the most conflicts about money, and the only person they might get along with is another person with a perfect score. Since we're not perfect, what can you do with your results that provides a true measurement of potential conflict? This is where the *financial compatibility matrix* comes into play.

First, let's go back and make sure you've completed the answer key correctly. Your responses for you and your partner should be included to correspond to your responses for each topic. To illustrate this, for topic 1, if Partner One (**P1**) responded true, they would enter a one (**1**), and if Partner Two (**P2**) responded false, they would enter a zero (**0**). Be sure to complete the answer key for all 41 topics. This is an important step in order to complete the next step.

P1: ________ **P2:** ________	**T**	**F**	**P1**	**P2**
1. My parents taught me about managing money.	1	0	1	0
2. My parents were careful about taking on debt.	1	0	0	1

Now that you've ensured that the answer key is complete, let's organize the topics in a way that more easily identifies areas for conflict and gives you a visual view of your financial compatibility with your partner.

The financial compatibility matrix (FCM) is composed of four quadrants. Each quadrant represents a combination of responses for Partner One (**P1**) and Partner Two (**P2**), represented as (**P1, P2**). The FCM organizes the topics into a view that identifies the topics that are more likely to cause conflict, allowing you to target these topics for additional review.

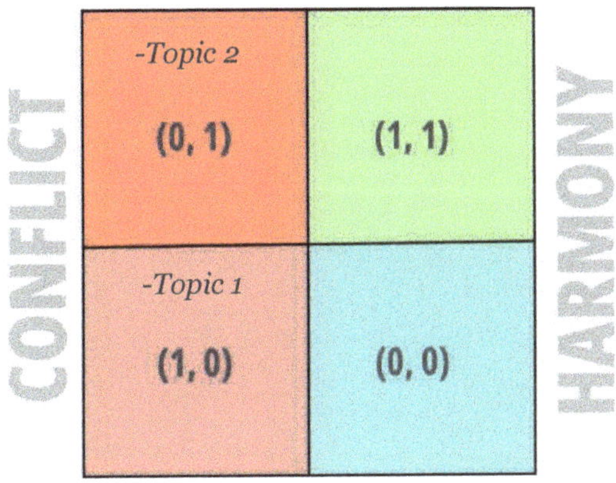

Bottom Left (1, 0): P1 agrees and P2 disagrees with the ideal response.
Top Left (0, 1): P1 disagrees and P2 agrees with the ideal response.
Top Right (1, 1): P1 and P2 agree with the ideal response.
Bottom Right (0, 0): P1 and P2 disagree with the ideal response.

All 41 topics should be placed in the matrix in a corresponding quadrant. The matrix should display all the topic numbers in two zones. The right side are topics where you will find harmony. Even though there may be some topics where you both did not agree with the ideal response, you still have agreement on your experience, approach, and sentiment. The left side of the matrix is the conflict zone. Here is where you may find that a different experience, approach, and sentiment could cause conflict. The conflict zone might as well be called the zone of opportunity because this is where you're going to focus your attention. Use the chart on the following page to complete your financial compatibility matrix, and refer to the matrix as you go through the topics.

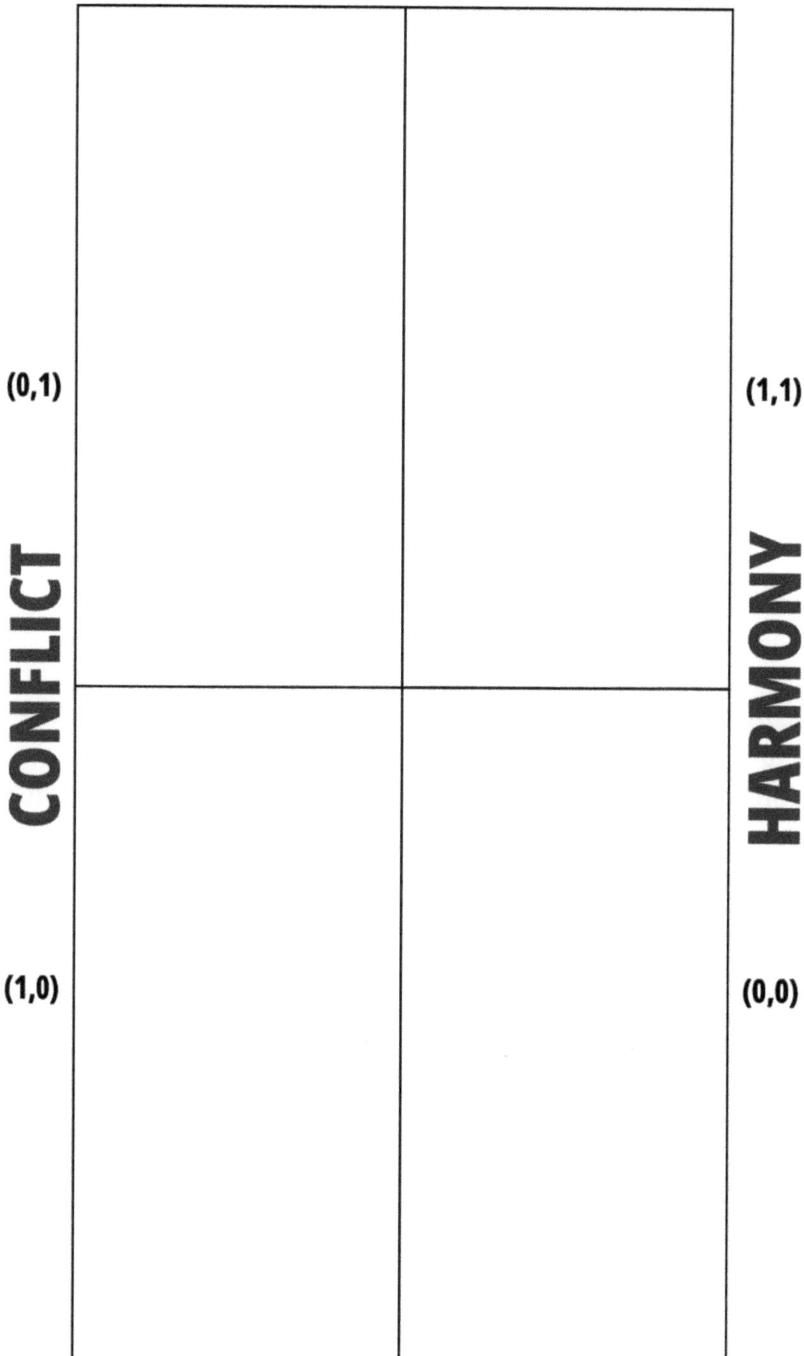
(0,1)
(1,1)
CONFLICT
HARMONY
(1,0)
(0,0)

EVALUATE AND REVIEW THE TOPICS

You've taken the assessment, tallied your scores, and created your financial compatibility matrix. Now, let's begin our journey of exploring each topic in the assessment and learning about why each topic is relevant and how it impacts your relationship with money and finances and your relationship with your partner. You will explore each topic using a three-part evaluation and review method:

1. ***Why it matters***
2. ***Why there's conflict***
3. ***Discussion points***

Why it matters

The first step takes a point of view of each topic and breaks down each topic to provide context around why the ideal perspective is so important. When it comes to finances, there is a right way and a wrong way to go about it. There rarely is an in between or grey area. Remember, the goal of this book is to help resolve conflict by clearing up any misconception and limiting beliefs around money and finances. The point of view that is provided is supported by ample research and examples pointing to the right way of approaching the topic. You may be slightly reluctant to accept the point of view being presented on a certain topic as the topic may be around a matter that you had no control of, especially in the beginning of the assessment, which deals with your parents' approach to managing money.

> ***"If you weren't part of an ideal situation growing up, this point of view is not meant to be an assault on your upbringing."***

The point of view is meant to provide a perspective of how your parents' habits and decisions surrounding their finances could have affected you, as well as to provide you with an understanding of why growing up or not growing up in the ideal circumstances matters.

Why there's conflict

Here is where we examine potential causes of conflict that could exist around each topic. We examine a scenario where you and your partner have differing responses to a given topic and how the difference in experience, approach, or sentiment to that topic could create potential conflict. The assumption that conflict could arise from a certain topic just from having different responses is justified, as the nature of the topics were determined to be more problematic, as discussed earlier in the book when we broke down the method behind the FCA. You may also find the you and your partner have the same response that is contrary to the ideal response and recommended perspective in the *Why It Matters* narrative. We recommend using this as an opportunity to avoid potential conflict and to embrace the ideal point of view as a learning opportunity.

Discussion points

Each topic includes suggested discussion points to help you and your partner resolve the conflict. We carefully curated the talking points to help directly address the specific reasons for conflict identified during the topic evaluation. Here is where the rubber meets the road. We've put together some key discussion topics to address how to avoid potential conflict, and how to resolve it if it already exists. Here is where you and your partner will take the time to have potentially difficult conversations. Use the discussion points as a guide to talk through the topics. Listen to each other and be empathetic to each other's experiences. Be transparent with one another and make efforts to understand each other's background.

PART ONE

YOUR EXPERIENCES WITH MONEY AND FINANCES GROWING UP

1

MY PARENTS TAUGHT ME ABOUT MANAGING MONEY

Growing up in a household where your parents taught you about managing money is ideal. The preferred response is true.

WHY IT MATTERS

If your parents taught you how to manage money, learning those skills at a young age was likely a huge advantage—and may have helped you make better financial decisions as an adult. Being knowledgeable in budgeting, saving, and the value of money likely helped you navigate the increasingly complex world of finances and may have helped you steer clear of unnecessary debt traps while maximizing your earning potential. Parents play a huge influence in teaching children how to manage their finances. Some of the good habits that are practiced in the home include learning to meet needs over wants, saving for the future, and goal setting. Such habits are beneficial in the long run as they help to improve stability and success. A study by the Federal Deposit Insurance Commission (FDIC) revealed the following insights: "Teaching kids about money early on will help them to become more financially independent as they get older. Financial education has been linked to lower debt levels, higher savings, and higher credit scores as children mature into adulthood." (6)

I remember my first lesson on managing money when my parents took me to the bank to open my very first savings account. They taught me how to keep track of the deposits and withdrawals using a small booklet that came with the account. The important lesson on saving has stuck with me, along with other lessons my parents taught me about managing money. These lessons have helped to shape my approach to finances, which I plan to teach my kids one day.

WHY THERE'S CONFLICT

Having been taught to manage money as a child gives you a leg up as an adult. This falls into the category of *experience*. Your partner, who may not have had similar opportunities to learn at a young age, may have a harder time navigating their finances. However, this may not be the case. Remember that while your experiences as a child may differ, your current approach as an adult is what matters. Your childhood gives a window into the adversities you may have had to overcome in order to become a functioning adult. Regardless of your background, you should be equipped with money management skills and knowledge, especially if you're planning to start a family of your own. These essential money management skills will help to ensure a bright and financially sound future for your family and ensure that the new generation is taught to manage money from an early age.

DISCUSSION POINTS

1. Discuss the lessons your parents taught you about managing money. Understanding each other's upbringing and experiences can help you recognize why you might have different perspectives.

2. Acknowledge and respect each other's differences, including cultural, familial, or personal traditions and values.

3. Talk about what drove you to learn about money management and how financial literacy has improved your relationship with money.

4 Discuss common goals that align with both backgrounds. Focusing on shared objectives can help bridge differences and create a sense of unity.

2

MY PARENTS WERE CAREFUL ABOUT TAKING ON DEBT

Growing up in a household where your parents were cautious about going into debt is ideal. The preferred response is true.

WHY IT MATTERS

It is wisest to be a bit cautious when it comes to debt, specifically when it comes to unnecessary personal debt. The accumulation of debt becomes an added burden that can quickly spiral out of control. Growing up, if your parents chose to control their finances and avoid wasting money and accumulating personal debt, they were more likely to create an environment at home that was more conducive to your development and overall well-being.

Excess personal debt has been shown to be harmful to children's socioemotional well-being, which includes the ability to empathize, communicate effectively, manage emotions, and navigate social situations, which are crucial skills for personal and interpersonal success. A study published in by the American Academics of Pediatrics in 2016 suggests the following: "Greater total debt was associated with poorer child socioemotional well-being. [...] Higher levels of home mortgage and education debt were associated with greater socioemotional well-being for children, whereas higher levels of and increases in unsecured debt were associated with lower levels of and declines in child socioemotional well-being" (7) While debt can be a source of stress, taking on certain types of debt responsibly, such as a mortgage or student loans that are used to improve the standard of living, provides a benefit for the family.

WHY THERE'S CONFLICT

Growing up with a perspective of debt that is different from your partner could place you at odds when the discussion of using debt comes up, even if the debt is used in a manner that is both responsible and beneficial. This falls into the category of *experience*. You may find that you are at odds with your partner, who has extremely negative views of debt because of how they observed their parent's irresponsible use of debt. No matter the childhood circumstances, it's important to acknowledge the possible impact on your current approach to debt because of your experience as a child.

DISCUSSION POINTS

1. Discuss how your parents' attitudes toward debt have influenced your own views.
2. Share your comfort levels regarding taking on debt. Some people are comfortable with certain types of debt (e.g., mortgages) but not others (e.g., credit card debt).
3. Talk about how differing views on debt could impact your relationship and how you can work together to find common ground.
4. Establish how you will communicate about financial decisions related to debt.
5. If necessary, talk about setting boundaries with extended family, especially if they might influence financial decisions or expectations around debt.

3

MY PARENTS HAD FREQUENT DISAGREEMENTS OVER HOW TO SPEND MONEY

Growing up seeing your parents having frequent disagreements over how to spend money was less than ideal. The preferred response is false.

WHY IT MATTERS

Disagreements between parents on the issue of money can be damaging to the family. Growing up in an environment where your parents had frequent disagreements about money may have caused you to have a negative association with money matters. "Witnessing frequent arguments or conflicts between parents can cause children to feel anxious, stressed, and even depressed. It can also affect their behavior, as they may act out in response to the conflict." (8) It's important for parents to learn how to handle their financial differences in a way that will not ruin the family bonds or harm the environment the child is growing up in.

When parents are on different pages regarding their finances, bad decisions are more common, like spending uncontrollably and not saving enough, which can be a great danger to the family. Children pick up financial habits that are taught by their parents, and constant arguments can cultivate negative perceptions of money and cause a lot of stress in the household. Furthermore, financial disputes may highlight other problems, such as mistrust or conflicting values, which will weaken family relationships and make it hard to attend to the children's needs.

WHY THERE'S CONFLICT

While this topic falls into the category of *experience,* you may find that conflicts arise from your approach when disagreements about money come up. Growing up without a good role model of how to work through disagreements and conflict is a direct link to an adult who has difficulty resolving conflicts, especially when it comes to finances. Conflicts arise as a result of a lack of effective communication about money matters. This lack of effective communication may be the root cause of many disagreements about money, and not having a good example growing up could have influenced you or your partner's approach to resolving differences.

DISCUSSION POINTS

1 If applicable, talk about how witnessing your parents' disagreements influenced your views on money and financial management.

2 If applicable, talk about how you witnessed your parents resolve their disagreements and how that influenced your approach to managing disagreements over money.

3 Discuss how you both prefer to communicate about finances. Establishing a healthy and open dialogue can prevent misunderstandings and help you address financial issues collaboratively.

4 Discuss what financial values are important to each of you, whether it's saving and investing, or spending on experiences. Embrace each other's values as you work toward your shared financial goals.

4

MY PARENTS EMPHASIZED THE NEED TO SAVE FOR EMERGENCIES

Growing up with parents who emphasized the need to save for emergencies is ideal. The preferred response is true.

WHY IT MATTERS

It is definitely the right move for parents to save for the unexpected. This allows children to feel financially secure. Seeing your parents put money aside for unforeseen circumstances definitely helped you understand that being prepared is essential for handling life's challenges. Through your parents, you are able to understand the reasons why you need to save money in order to meet unexpected needs. You saw firsthand the efforts your parents made to protect the family's financial well-being. You were likely aware that through your parent's efforts, the family was better prepared to face a variety of challenges.

In my household growing up, I was always told to "save for a rainy day," and to this day, that idiom sticks with me, along with "when it rains, it pours." My dad was the main character in my life who advocated for saving as much as possible. He believed wholeheartedly that saving was a way to gain financial freedom. Personal finance "expert" Dave Ramsey shares the same idea. His belief system revolves around maximizing savings and eliminating debt. I'm not here to endorse Mr. Ramsey, as I don't agree with all of his methods. However, I do agree that you must place great emphasis on savings, and the first thing you ought to do is establish your emergency fund.

WHY THERE'S CONFLICT

The stress of wondering how your parents are going to foot the bill for an emergency situation has a profound effect on a child. If you experienced this in childhood, it likely influenced how you approach savings as an adult. Are you an adult who values saving money despite your parents not putting an emphasis on saving? Or, are you an adult who does not put emphasis on saving money because your parents did not put emphasis on saving? Conflict can arise when you and your partner do not share the same values on saving money, and these values usually stem from childhood.

DISCUSSION POINTS

1. Discuss how your childhood experience may have influenced your current views on saving for emergencies.

2. If applicable, talk about how the difference in upbringing may have influenced your values when it comes to having adequate savings.

3. Discuss what constitutes an emergency, and when it's appropriate to dip into your savings.

4. Talk about the importance of prioritizing saving money over non-essential expenses. This might involve making lifestyle adjustments to free up more money for your emergency fund.

5

I GREW UP IN A DUAL-INCOME HOUSEHOLD

Growing up in a dual income household is ideal.
The preferred response is true.

WHY IT MATTERS

Growing up in a dual-income household may have provided several advantages that contribute to financial stability, personal development, and overall well-being. If you grew up with two sources of income, you were more likely to have an increased level of financial stability. It is not always easy to raise children in a family where both parents work. There are a number of factors that would inhibit that from being possible. First, we need to distinguish between the two forms of single-earner households, which are single-parent single-income household and dual-parent single-income household. Both are very different circumstances and provide different outcomes in comparison to dual-parent dual-income households.

For starters, children who grow up in a single-parent household are inherently at a disadvantage. Aside from not having the intrinsic benefits of having both parents in the home, children from single-parent households often are more disadvantaged academically and ultimately financially. (9) Again, this is not an attack on anyone's childhood experience. There is indeed many benefits to having a strong single parent, and a special award needs to be given to all single parents. They are the real MVPs. This is just a book trying to explain why your unique experience could potentially be at odds with someone else's unique experience. It's simply a comparison to the advantages that a person from a dual-parent dual-income household might have had.

When it comes to dual-parent single-income households, there is much debate over whether this approach is better for the child developmentally when compared to a dual-income household. There are indeed pros and cons to both situations. For our purposes, we will combine both forms of two parent households together. So, if you grew up in a dual-parent single-income household and you initially entered a **0** for this topic, congratulations, you may change your response to **1**. However, you're not out of the conflict zone yet! There's still a likelihood of conflict no matter which quadrant you put this particular topic in your compatibility matrix.

WHY THERE'S CONFLICT

When it comes to this topic, the conflict amongst couples comes down to the type of dual-parent household you and your partner want to provide for your children. This is a unique topic where in many cases, your experience influences your sentiment and drives your approach. It more often comes down to making the choice between having a dual-earner versus a single-earner household. This conflict really comes down to values and lifestyle. On one hand, your values, whether familial or cultural, could influence your preference for a single-earner household. This used to be considered the more "traditional" household. However, at this point in society, we might as well call that ancient history. Lifestyle has a lot to do with the decline of the single-earner household. The cost of living and other factors have forced the need for two-income households, which is now the more common family structure. Whatever the choice, it's important that each partner be on the same page. It's often difficult to compromise on one's values, so couples should ensure alignment on each other's values prior to taking the relationship to the next level. Making the choice between having a one or two-earner family comes down to lifestyle choices and affordability. No matter the choice, it should always be about making the right financial decision for your current or future family.

For the next generation, no matter the choice, seeing both parents contributing to the household will be a child's first example of shared responsibilities in action. It will enable them to see that both partners are equally contributing to the family's objectives. We still give the edge to dual income households as, statistically speaking, dual-income households are far likely to be able to provide for needs and wants, such as children's activities, enhanced education, and leisure travels, making for a more enriched childhood. A dual-income household may be a good way of helping children grow up being exposed to more egalitarian or equal gender roles. This view may influence the ideas they have about gender roles in their own relationships. Growing up with two working parents will also expose children to different career paths and professional experiences, which can expand their understanding of work and inspire them as they plan their futures.

DISCUSSION POINTS

1. How did growing up in a single-income or dual-income household shape your views on money, budgeting, and lifestyle choices?

2. Discuss whether you both expect to maintain a dual-income setup or if one of you might eventually prefer to focus on other pursuits, such as further education or staying home with children.

3. Discuss how you can create a budget that considers both of your financial contributions and lifestyle preferences. This can help ensure that both partners feel comfortable and supported.

4. How can having two incomes provide more financial freedom and opportunities? How can each person in the partnership maintain independence within a shared financial framework?

5 How can you leverage two incomes to boost savings and investments? Consider setting joint financial goals, such as saving for a house, retirement, or other long-term objectives.

6 Discuss how you can manage financial risks with two incomes, such as by building an emergency fund or obtaining insurance to cover potential loss of income.

7 Consider how having two incomes might impact work-life balance. Discuss any concerns about stress, workload, or time management, and how you can support each other in achieving a healthy balance.

8 What are each partner's career aspirations, and how can you support each other's professional growth? Discuss how career changes or advancements might impact your financial situation.

9 Discuss how to fairly divide household responsibilities, considering both partners' work commitments. This can help prevent potential conflicts and ensure a balanced partnership.

6

MY PARENTS SET GOALS FOR THE THINGS THEY NEEDED TO PURCHASE

Growing up with parents who had established goals of what they needed to purchase is ideal. The preferred response is <u>true</u>.

WHY IT MATTERS

It was definitely advantageous for you if your parents set goals for what they needed to purchase, as goal-oriented financial decision-making fosters stability, discipline, and a positive model for good spending habits. Having clear goals for purchases not only helped to ensure that your family's needs were met but also created a foundation of financial responsibility that likely benefited you in the long run. Your parents likely made every effort to prioritize necessities over impulsive spending. As a child, I often said to myself, "There are all these delicious options on every aisle, and all my mom seems to focus on is her grocery list." It was almost like she had blinders when she went grocery shopping. It was a good thing because the blinders helped my parents stick to their budget and ensured that money was used purposefully, and it served as one of my first lessons on healthy spending habits. I didn't know it at the time, but this goal-oriented spending habit helped to ensure that primary needs, such as housing, education, and healthcare, were prioritized. Hence, growing up and observing this goal-oriented spending habit taught me the importance of setting priorities and making thoughtful financial choices.

WHY THERE'S CONFLICT

Spending habits are a common source of conflict, and the FCA includes several topics addressing them. One such topic—setting spending goals—is divided into two parts. The first explores how your parents approached spending goals, while the second, covered in Topic 17, looks at your current approach. To understand potential conflict around spending habits, it helps to examine the root cause. Lacking a positive role model doesn't automatically lead to poor financial habits in adulthood, but it may help explain why some struggle with managing their spending.

As previously stated, parents play a significant role in shaping the habits of their children through their own habits, good or bad. Your experience would likely influence your approach, and we tested that assumption when you were asked about your current approach to spending in Topic 17. Conflict could arise from a difference in what it means to have good spending habits. For example, you and your partner may claim to have good spending habits, but your approach to spending may be different. Your upbringing could help to explain the difference in your approach to whether or not you had a good role model.

DISCUSSION POINTS

1 Discuss how your upbringing may have influenced your spending habits.

2 Discuss how your parents prioritize purchases based on needs versus wants, and how that influenced your approach.

3 Discuss what your parents did to minimize impulse spending, and how that influenced your approach.

7

MY PARENTS OFTEN FACED FINANCIAL DIFFICULTIES

Growing up with parents who seemed to always have financial difficulties is less than ideal. The preferred response is false.

WHY IT MATTERS

Growing up in a household where parents consistently faced financial difficulties may have presented several challenges that impacted your emotional, mental, and social development. While growing up in a household that experienced financial difficulty can instill resilience and resourcefulness, the emotional, educational, and social challenges it presents can have lasting effects. "Income instability is likely to interfere with healthy development, particularly if parents do not have the economic or psychological resources to maintain parenting practices and consistent spending on goods that promote children's well-being." (10) Financial difficulties often create tension and stress within the household. This tension can make children feel insecure or helpless about the family's situation, as they can often tell when their parents are anxious. In some cases, this early awareness may make children feel like they are being pushed to shoulder adult responsibilities, like having to work from an early age or even help support family expenses.

While taking on adult responsibilities at a young age can build resilience, it may also interfere with their education and childhood.

Watching parents struggle to make ends meet can be emotionally burdensome for children, who may internalize their parents' stress or feel responsible for alleviating it. Amongst other emotions, kids feel a sense of guilt for not being able to help. (11) Additionally, parents dealing with constant financial difficulties may have been unable to model effective money management behavior. This lack of positive financial behavior can leave children without the tools or knowledge to handle finances successfully as adults.

WHY THERE'S CONFLICT

Extensive research shows that growing up in a household with constant financial uncertainty can have a lasting impact. These children who grow up to be adults may be more risk-averse when it comes to finances and have a greater emotional response attached to money matters. Let's examine a very interesting study on the outcome of growing up with financial uncertainty. The study, published by the *Journal of Personality and Social Psychology*, showed the following findings: "Economic uncertainty leads people from poor childhoods to become more impulsive, while leading people from wealthy childhoods to become less impulsive." (12) An example of an impulsive individual in this context could be a person who is more likely to pick a quick fix or a short-term solution to a problem rather than a well thought-out, more long-term solution.

In addition, researchers found that adults who grew up in poverty were more likely to perceive difficult and uncertain living conditions as beyond their control, whereas those from wealthy backgrounds viewed them as within their control (12) These findings are especially interesting because in times of adversity, when reminded of their circumstances growing up, individuals from poorer backgrounds may feel like the situation is not within their control, so they may be less inclined to work and find a proper solution to the problem. This is where the conflict could come in. Conflict could even arise before financial problems arise.

During the process of working together to create a financial plan, you may find that your partner is less willing to discuss financial matters if the process reminds them of their difficult childhood. In effect, constant exposure to financial difficulties can shape a person's relationship with money. They may grow up with a fear of financial instability and avoid discussions about money while struggling to plan for the future.

The other factor that could cause conflict comes when you have a difference in the perception of financial risk from your partner. As I mentioned a moment ago, research indicates that adults who experienced financial difficulties growing up may be more risk-averse when it comes to finances and have a greater emotional response attached to money matters. Accordingly, research on people who have spent a lot of time at the bottom of the socioeconomic scale suggests that this experience makes people more cautious rather than more prone to taking risks; it appears that having few resources makes people more frugal with what they have and more inclined to make safe decisions in life. (13) In other words, the prevalence of financial difficulties as a child may translate to an increase in risk-averse behavior, such as not being willing to invest in stocks, start a business, or participate in any potentially beneficial activity that involves money. This immense fear of financial difficulty, while warranted, can be somewhat debilitating and prevent a person from doing things that could benefit them financially.

Conversely, the more financially advantaged your childhood was, the more likely you are to take on financial risk. The willingness to take financial risks is strongly and positively linked to childhood socioeconomic status. This suggests that early life conditions directly and profoundly influence economic choices and attitudes in adulthood. (14) One partner may prioritize financial security and be more focused on building savings or paying off debt, while the other partner might prioritize riskier investments. The difference in childhood circumstances could also impact life decisions. One partner might be more risk-averse when it comes to career changes, and conversations that come up around career moves could be difficult. In contrast, the other partner may be more willing to take advantage of opportunities that may present a risk if there is a financial benefit in return. These differences in attitudes towards financial risk will be a point of contention that couples will need to reconcile in order to minimize conflict.

DISCUSSION POINTS

1. If applicable, talk about how your parents' financial struggles have shaped your views on money and financial security.

2. Discuss what financial security means to each of you and how you can work together to achieve a stable financial future.

3. Discuss your willingness to take on financial risk and how that willingness or lack thereof has shaped your view of finances.

4. Discuss ways you can work together to address each other's tolerance to risk while creating a financial plan that meets both your needs.

8

MY PARENTS CREATED A BUDGET TO LIVE ON AND FOLLOWED IT

Growing up with parents who created a budget to live on and followed it is ideal. The preferred response is true.

WHY IT MATTERS

When it comes to household finances, a budget is at the center of the financial planning process. It's a window into your finances and a tool to help you manage your money. "How well you manage your budget can determine your ability to meet financial obligations and goals." (3) If your parents created a budget to live on, you likely saw this in action through your parents' behavior. They monitored expenses and were mindful of discretionary spending. You were aware that there were limits, and they made it very apparent when it came to wasteful behavior, like leaving the lights on or the water running. What you might have thought was constant nagging about how expensive things were was their way of managing the budget.

This budget-conscious mindset likely provided you with several benefits. It helped shape positive habits and attitudes that may have influenced your own approach to money management. It also provided you with your parents' version of thoughtful financial management, even if it sounded like nagging. The bottom line is your parents ensured that you grew up with the skills and mindset needed to successfully navigate your own financial journey. Budgeting is a fundamental skill that teaches responsibility, organization, and planning. These skills are transferable to other areas of life and contribute to overall success and well-being.

WHY THERE'S CONFLICT

If you did not observe your parents living on a budget, you were more likely to follow a similar habit and "fly by the seat of your pants," no matter your socioeconomic status. Poor financial habits are a primary catalyst for arguments over money. Along with poor spending habits and debt management, not incorporating a budget increases the chance of money mismanagement and the likelihood of conflict with your partner. It is important to note that if you didn't observe your parents living on a budget, it does not mean that you don't currently live on a budget. We will explore your current approach in Topic 13. While this topic focuses on your experience, which could have influenced your approach, Topic 13 will take a deeper dive into your current approach to budgeting and cover more specific issues that create conflict.

DISCUSSION POINTS

There is definitely value in discussing your experiences growing up and observing your parents' approach to managing finances. Whether or not you observed your parents managing a budget, it is worthwhile to engage with your partner about how your experience may have shaped your approach as an adult.

1. If applicable, talk about how growing up without a budget may have influenced your views on money management.

2. If applicable, discuss the advantages of growing up with a budget, such as having control over finances, reduced stress, achieving financial goals, and avoiding debt.

9

MY PARENTS SHOPPED AROUND FOR THE BEST DEAL BEFORE MAKING A PURCHASE

Growing up with parents who spent time shopping for a good deal before making a purchase is ideal. The preferred response is true.

WHY IT MATTERS

Good spending habits are hard to come by, so if your parents made the effort to shop for a good deal before making a purchase, you were fortunate to observe a trait that helped set you on the right course. Observing your parents spend time shopping for a good deal provided valuable lessons in financial responsibility and critical thinking, and it likely provided you with lifelong skills like thoughtful decision-making and a greater appreciation for the value of money. Watching your parents compare prices and look for the best deals likely instilled the importance of getting the most bang for the buck.

As a personal testimony, I recall my dad wanting to build a new stereo system in the summer of 1996. I stayed with him for the summer, and we loved music and getting the best possible sound experience. We set off to go shopping for two 10-inch sub-woofers to replace the old sub-woofers in the set of speaker boxes we were refurbishing. We set off one afternoon and went to the first stereo shop. My dad narrowed down the specific brand and model he wanted: a set of Pioneer speakers that he knew could do the job and work well acoustically in the newly refurbished speaker boxes. He asked for the price and negotiated down as much as he could. We finally landed on a price, only for my dad to say that he would think about it, and then he left. I was a bit confused because I thought we had the sales guy right where we wanted him to be price-wise.

As we walked back to the car, we passed where we parked, turned down the street, and walked right into another stereo store where we saw the exact same sub-woofers. My dad told the salesperson that we got a price at another store, upon which the salesperson said he would not only match the price but beat it. My dad said thanks and left once again. He went to a third store with a new lower price in hand, and low and behold, the store matched and beat that price. My dad, feeling confident with the price, proceeded to make his purchase. I asked my dad what had just happened, and he smiled and said that he had an amount in his head that he was willing to spend, and that amount was met. I joked and said we probably could have gone to another store. He smirked and said perhaps, but there was no sense in being greedy. I definitely learned some valuable lessons that day. Observing this deal hunting process helped me understand the importance of taking the time to find a good deal, as well as the significance of patience and delayed gratification. Being exposed to this process made me more likely to adopt similar strategies in adulthood. I learned to avoid impulsive buying and to prioritize well-considered purchases.

WHY THERE'S CONFLICT

Parents play a significant role in shaping the spending habits of their children through their own spending habits, good or bad. Shopping for a good deal is something we all should appreciate. Unfortunately, not everyone appreciates the process of finding a good deal. Conflict can arise when partners don't share the same level of enthusiasm and interest in finding the best deal. One partner may feel comfortable shopping for the same brand items on a grocery list, while another may want to shop different brands each time to ensure the best price. One partner may shop at the same place for home supplies while another may want to ensure they go to the store with the best price for that particular item. One partner may be bothered by overspending on an item even if it's one dollar, while the other partner may not be so price sensitive.

DISCUSSION POINTS

Whether or not we observed our parents practicing the habit of shopping around for a good deal shouldn't stop us from doing the same. I think we can all agree that getting the best value for our money is the way to go, but it doesn't have to be as complicated as walking around to three different stereo shops to find a good deal.

1. Talk about how your parents' approach to shopping has influenced your current spending habits and attitudes toward money. Understanding each other's background can help you navigate discussions more effectively.

2. Discuss the advantages of shopping for deals, such as saving money, getting better value for your purchases, and stretching your budget further.

3. Talk about the importance of researching products and prices before making a purchase. Discuss strategies for comparing prices online, reading reviews, and seeking recommendations.

4. Discuss the benefits of timing purchases to coincide with sales, promotions, or clearance events. This might involve planning major purchases around holiday sales or end-of-season discounts.

5. Talk about differentiating between needs and wants when shopping. Discuss how prioritizing needs can help focus spending on essential items and avoid unnecessary purchases.

6. Discuss strategies to control impulse buying, such as implementing a waiting period before making non-essential purchases or setting aside a "fun money" budget for discretionary spending

7 What are some ways that both partners can feel a sense of satisfaction for finding a good a deal? Find ways to celebrate the wins by focusing on the end results instead of the process.

10

MY PARENTS WERE CAUTIOUS ABOUT USING CREDIT CARDS

Growing up with parents who were cautious with their use of credit cards is ideal. The preferred response is true.

WHY IT MATTERS

Credit cards and credit card usage have increased significantly over the years. In fact, they are the most common type of debt in the U.S. By the end of 2022, Americans owed an all-time high of $986 billion on credit cards. (15) Credit cards have been ingrained in our society as necessary, but it wasn't always this way, as a lot of our parents and grandparents had a very different attitude toward credit cards. My mom, for example, understood the importance of responsible credit card use and saw a credit card as a tool to help provide financial flexibility, providing an option in the chance of unexpected emergencies or managing large purchases. On the other hand, my dad saw credit cards as something to avoid and used only if absolutely necessary, such as in an emergency. He believed in cash and made it a point to remind me of it every chance he got.

Needless to say, my mom may have been right on this one. She is a retired mathematician who taught me how to do my taxes, so this makes sense. Our parents' use of credit cards can shape our own usage and habits. Choosing to use credit cards responsibly or not isn't a simple decision we make; it's a process that often starts with the influence of our parents. While learning through observation provides some initial benefits, observation without proper guidance can lead to irresponsible credit card use, and irresponsible credit card use is the gateway drug to debt mismanagement, and we all know how slippery of a slope this can be.

WHY THERE'S CONFLICT

As stated before, poor spending habits are a primary catalyst for conflict. A credit card is the primary tool of choice for bad spending habits. "A lack of positive role models for responsible credit card use during childhood can be a root cause of conflict in this area. Taking time to understand each other's financial background can help resolve these issues and support the development of a compatibility plan—one that promotes financial literacy and compensates for gaps left by early parental examples. We start the conversation of credit card use in the FCA with this topic, as it is a window into your own attitudes and approach. There will be lots of discussion when it comes to the differences between your and your partner's use of credit cards.

DISCUSSION POINTS

1. If applicable, talk about how your parents' credit card usage has influenced your use of credit cards and debt.
2. If applicable, discuss your parents views on using credit cards when you were growing up.
3. If applicable, discuss if your parents allowed to use their credit card and what lessons this taught you.
4. If applicable, talk about any strategies your parents' may have adopted for managing and reducing credit card debt.
5. Discuss whether or not your parents, taught you the importance of credit and managing your credit score.

11

MY PARENTS USED COUPONS

Growing up with parents who used coupons is ideal.
The preferred response is <u>true</u>.

WHY IT MATTERS

When I think of coupons, I often get the vision of the *Extreme Couponing* reality television show (16), where shoppers take saving money to the next level through radical coupon clipping and savvy shopping skills. The more realistic recollection for me is a vision of my mom's miscellaneous drawer in the kitchen that was stuffed with paper coupons, most of which were expired. Believe it or not, if your parents used coupons, they actually provided several practical and educational benefits that contributed to your family's financial health. The mere act of clipping and saving coupons can teach valuable life lessons, regardless of your socioeconomic status. Parents who used coupons were more likely to have managed family finances well and provided their children with essential skills and a common-sense approach to saving money. As a child growing up, the most common use of coupons was to reduce the cost of groceries and household items. My parents made every effort to get the best price for things such as groceries. I would observe my mom handing the cashier coupons, and the cashier would announce the savings amount. They would even honor some of those expired coupons. This practice of saving coupons still lingers with me today as I find the need to save random coupons that come in the mail, regardless if I ever use them or not.

WHY THERE'S CONFLICT

Coupon usage is another one of those traits that is often passed down. If your parents shopped for bargains through coupons or other methods, then you likely picked up that habit. The opposite is also true, and if your parents didn't care to use coupons, then it's likely you don't either. "Seeing money spent frivolously, they learn frivolous spending. Similarly, if they see Mom and Dad using coupons and watching for sale items, comparing prices and openly discussing how family money is spent, then children will learn more careful, thoughtful habits." (17)

So, what if your partner did not grow up observing this behavior? Well, it may not necessarily mean they don't care about saving money, as using coupons isn't the only way to save. However, the learned behavior of looking for savings might be something that your partner is not as well-versed in, and this might present some conflict as you may feel that a better deal might have existed had your partner simply taken the time to look.

DISCUSSION POINTS

1. Discuss how growing up with or without the use of coupons has influenced your views on shopping and saving.

2. If applicable, talk about the advantages you observed from your parents using coupons.

3. If applicable, talk about the process your parents took to collect and use coupons.

4. If applicable, talk about the conversations your parents had with you or the lessons they taught you about using coupons.

12

MY PARENTS PAID THE BILLS ON TIME

Growing up with parents who always paid the bills on time is ideal. The preferred response is true.

WHY IT MATTERS

We've seen the impact of growing up with financial difficulties and the impact that it can have on your childhood and as an adult. We've focused on observations of good financial habits for the last four topics. The habit of paying bills on time is the final topic in the FCA dealing with your childhood observations. This topic is especially important for several reasons. For starters, if you grew up in a home where your parents paid the bills on time, then you likely benefited from financial, emotional, and educational advantages. These advantages include greater financial stability, a less stressful home environment, and early lessons on responsible money management.

We've talked extensively about your parent's spending habits, and for good reason! Elizabeth Gravier of CNBC interviewed Mac Gardner, a financial literacy advocate for young children. He states that the number one behavior children learn from their parents is spending habits. (18) Responsible spending habits are a big deal, but so is paying your bills on time. While we all agree that it is important to pay our bills on time, this is the one behavior that was less likely to be observed growing up, as our parents tended to do this behind closed doors. I personally never recalled an instance where my parents sat me down and explained to me the process of paying the light bill, even though they certainly talked about the light bill quite frequently, especially if I left a light on.

Growing up, paying bills was seen as a grown-up activity, much like all of the financial responsibilities our parents had. They likely believed we were not mature enough to understand this responsibility as children. We were told that bills needed to be paid, but we weren't shown how. It could be that they didn't want to burden us with the stress they felt or maybe they saw bills as a private matter. Whatever the reason, times have not changed much, as there is still a general hesitancy to discuss finances. According to the 14th annual T. Rowe Price Parents, Kids & Money Survey conducted in January 2022, 57 percent of parents surveyed have at least some reluctance to discuss money matters with their kids. (19)

WHY THERE'S CONFLICT

If you were fortunate enough to not only see your parents paying the bills but to have been educated on the process at an early age, then you were given a head start on responsible money management. Since you learned the importance of prioritizing needs over wants in order to ensure financial stability, you were more likely to adopt these habits in your own adult lives. So, what if your partner was not so fortunate? How do you co-exist with a partner who seems to be a bit cavalier with due dates for bills? Conflict around your parent's approach to bills often escalated from circumstances such as a missed payment due to a simple oversight or issues related to outright habitual late payments. Arguments about the bills, such as who pays what and when, rank among the top reasons couples fight about money, according to a study in the *Journal of Social and Personal Relationships*. (20) We can definitely learn from our parent's approach and look at ways to incorporate good habits and eliminate bad ones.

DISCUSSION POINTS

You and your partner need to have a good conversation about your experiences growing up before discussing your current approach to managing your bills. Understanding each other's experiences will greatly aid in identifying and addressing potential conflict with your partner and help preserve the well-being of your finances and your relationship.

1. Talk about the levels of exposure each of you had to observing your parents paying the bills.
2. Discuss how your parents' approach to paying bills has influenced your views on money management and financial responsibility.
3. Talk about any lack of exposure to your parents' approach and how that influenced your views on money management and financial responsibility.
4. If applicable, discuss why your parents emphasized paying the bills on time.
5. If applicable, discuss the benefits you observed from knowing your parents paid the bills on time.
6. If applicable, talk about how you felt when your parents could not pay the bills on time.
7. If applicable, discuss whether you observed your parents having disagreements about bills. How did they resolve their disagreements?
8. Discuss what you wished your parents had taught you regarding managing bills and how it could have helped you in adulthood.
9. Discuss how you would approach the topic of bills differently with your children.

PART TWO

YOUR CURRENT PRACTICES AND BELIEFS ABOUT MONEY AND FINANCES

13

I HAVE A BUDGET AND LIVE WITHIN IT

Having a budget and living within it is ideal.
The preferred response is true.

WHY IT MATTERS

Let's discuss your approach to budgeting and how it may differ from your partner's approach. The difference in approach is what often leads to conflict. At the heart of the discussion is the importance of a budget. As discussed previously, a budget is an important component of your financial planning process. It's a window into your finances and a tool to help you manage your money. When we hear the word budget, we often think of restrictions and guardrails. While this is inherently true, a budget is much more. It's about creating stability and making progress toward your personal and financial goals.

So, how important is it really to incorporate a formal budget? Well, a statement from my book *Marriage & Finances* sums it up best: "Creating a budget is an important step in managing your household finances effectively. A budget plan helps you track your income and expenses, identify areas where you can save money, and achieve your financial goals." (3) While I realize some of you may not be married yet, it goes without saying that a budget benefits individual and joint households. Your budget helps to ensure that essential expenses like housing, food, and utilities are met, reducing the risk of financial instability. Your budget forces you to evaluate your spending habits, helps you prioritize needs over wants, and helps you avoid impulse purchases. Last but not least, your budget can be used as a planning tool to provide a clear roadmap for turning long-term aspirations into achievable outcomes.

WHY THERE'S CONFLICT

There is a distinct difference between individuals who incorporate a formal budget and those that don't. I have always systematically planned my life around a budget. I even created my own budget database tool 15 years ago because I wasn't quite satisfied with the tools that were available at the time. I still use that tool to this day. Now obviously I'm a bit of a personal finance nerd, but my wife on the other hand, well let's just say I never quite understood how she managed to live life without a formal budget. Before we got married, we had quite a few conversations about our finances, and when she told me that she managed her finances by simply monitoring her online bank statements, I scratched my head in bewilderment and disbelief.

I recognized that one of the main sources of conflict around budgeting is the different ways we think about and manage money. Just because my soon-to-be wife hadn't created a formal budget herself didn't mean she wasn't living within one. That realization has stayed with me over the years and helped me to be more understanding of her method. That didn't mean that her way was full proof and couldn't use a few pointers, but it did mean that I needed to acknowledge her process before I could even dream of attempting to suggest ways she could improve. Luckily for me, she was very open to improving her finances and I gladly helped her. A very common issue that often causes conflicts comes from having a poorly developed budget, one that fails to include key expenses or planned purchases. This creates issues when those purchases do come up. A poorly developed budget is like a partial map that you're relying on to get from point A to point B. Oftentimes, this originates from a lack of clear communication about crucial expenses or purchases that should have been included in order to present a complete picture of your budget plan.

The next aspect of budgeting, and the most obvious thing that can cause conflict, comes from the lack of living by a budget. If you or your partner lack a clear understanding of what it means to live on a budget—regardless of your socioeconomic background—it will inevitably lead to challenges. We've already discussed the importance of healthy spending habits, and your budget is the foundation that supports them. Without financial control, chaos can spill into both your personal life and your relationships. "Some of the most common reasons for divorce include communication and relationship quality issues, but money disagreements are right up there." (21) Acceptance and taking accountability for your own actions related to a lack of control is an absolute crucial first step in addressing the reason for conflict with your partner. Without this acknowledgment, your partner's denial can become a constant source of frustration, leading to frequent arguments and putting strain on the relationship.

The last area that could cause conflict involves the actual process of developing your budget. Creating a joint budget comes with its share of complications that could lead to arguments. Deciding what to prioritize in your budget requires compromise. Getting over the hurdle of creating a joint budget that is beneficial for both you and your partner is crucial, as a clear budget provides transparency, reduces misunderstandings, and fosters better communication and trust. "Working together as a team to manage your household budget and striving toward a common objective is a great display of partnership and teamwork." (3)

DISCUSSION POINTS

1 Start by sharing each other's current approach to managing your monthly finances. Understanding each other's habits and attitudes can provide insight into why they might or might not have a budget.

2 Talk about the advantages of budgeting, such as gaining better control over finances, reducing financial stress, achieving

savings goals, and having a clear picture of where money is going.

3 Discuss how having a budget can help you achieve your short-term and long-term financial goals.

4 Work together to create a shared budget that includes income, essential expenses (like rent, utilities, and groceries), and discretionary spending. Look into using online software or budgeting apps.

5 Discuss some common budgeting challenges, such as underestimating expenses or not accounting for irregular expenses, and how to address them.

6 Discuss setting spending limits for different categories to ensure that you stay within your means and avoid overspending.

14

I USE COUPONS

Incorporating the use of coupons into your finances is ideal. The preferred response is true.

WHY IT MATTERS

The benefits of coupons are obvious; finding a deal, whether it's through a coupon or a sale, is a valuable life skill. A quick history of coupons reveals that coupons, like sales, were created by retailers with the intention to drive sales. Attractive offers tend to drive people to make a purchase even if they don't need the item they purchased. So, what does coupon use look like from a modern-day perspective? "In 2020, 88 percent of survey respondents in the United States stated that they had used coupons for shopping." (22) In a world of online retail shopping, we've seen a shift from physical coupons to digital coupons, appealing to the younger demographic of online shoppers. "According to the March 2018 findings, 53.8 percent of internet users ranging between the ages of 18 and 29 years stated that discounts and coupons were a very important feature in the overall digital purchasing decision, while in comparison, only 34.3 percent of users aged 60 years and above stated the same." (23)

While physical coupons still exist, digital coupons have become a more widespread medium for savings. Digital coupons directly from the retailer or manufacturer, along with third-party websites and apps, are common. According to Statista, in 2018, 71 percent of all U.S. adults looked for coupons directly on store websites (24). So, what does all this data show? It highlights just how important coupons are in the pursuit of savings—on par with sales and other bargain opportunities. But we're not here to talk specifically about coupons, as the important aspect of the topic of coupons isn't really the coupons themselves but the spending habits you adopt in the pursuit of saving money. Hence, for this topic, we'll replace "coupons" with the term "smart shopping." So, let's review the benefits of coupons or, should I say, smart shopping.

Smart shopping offers a number of financial and practical benefits, providing a way to save money while fostering valuable life skills. Smart shopping takes some level of effort to seek out savings opportunities and make the most of available resources. It heightens awareness of the cost of items, helping you to become more intentional about your purchases and avoid overspending. It encourages you to spend thoughtfully and focus on discounts for items you want or need, giving you the best bang for your buck. With smart shopping, you will develop spending habits that can positively impact both your short-term and long-term financial goals. With all the benefits of smart shopping, why would couples fight over savings? Seems impossible, yet this is an area where a lot of conflict occurs.

WHY THERE'S CONFLICT

We know the benefits of coupons, smart shopping, and saving money in today's world, which has definitely progressed from the days of collecting expired coupons in a kitchen drawer. With all the tools at our disposal, you would think that shopping around for the best deal would be automatic, and everyone would take advantage of it. Unfortunately, this isn't the case. "Conflicts in a relationship can come about when partners have different approaches to spending and saving." (25) One partner might view smart shopping as a practical and savvy way to manage their finances, finding great satisfaction in finding a bargain and the accomplishment that comes with saving money. On the other hand, one partner may see the process of smart shopping as way too time-consuming or even unnecessary, preferring to prioritize convenience over spending additional time looking for a bargain that might not even exist. This difference in attitudes can lead to frustration, especially if one partner feels judged or undervalued for their approach to money management. This frustration can also lead to bigger arguments about spending habits and could serve as a gateway to other differences between you and your partner.

DISCUSSION POINTS

Conflicts around smart shopping are easier to identify and solve if you and your partner are focused on becoming more financially compatible. Discussing the topic and developing a path to compatibility is paramount.

1 If applicable, talk about why you or your partner may see smart shopping as inconvenient and not worth the time.

2 Talk about how smart shopping has become more accessible with digital options. Many stores offer apps or websites where you can easily find and use coupons without clipping paper versions.

3 Discuss simple ways to incorporate smart shopping into your routine, such as checking for digital coupons before grocery shopping or using apps that automatically apply discounts.

4 Discuss how to incorporate smart shopping without compromising on the quality of products. Emphasize using coupons for items you already plan to buy.

5 Talk about the potential pitfall of buying unnecessary items just because there's on discount or sale. Focus on using smart shopping for regularly purchased items or needs.

6 Share any positive experiences or savings achieved through smart shopping. Hearing about successful savings can be motivating.

7 Broaden the conversation to include other types of savings, like cashback apps, loyalty programs, and sales, to maximize your savings strategy.

8 Talk about balancing the desire to save money with the need for quality products. There may be instances where the cheapest option may not provide the best value.

9 Discuss whether savings from smart shopping could be allocated to other areas, such as a fun activity, saving and investing, or paying down debt.

15

I PAY MY BILLS ON TIME EACH MONTH

Paying your bills on time each month is ideal. The preferred response is true.

WHY IT MATTERS

Paying your bills on time each month is one of the first signs of a person who is financially fit. It reflects a personal commitment to financial responsibility and builds trust with your service providers, lenders, and landlords. It helps to create a good track record with your lenders, helping to improve your credit score. Timely payments help to avoid additional costs, such as late fees and penalties, and to prevent issues such as service interruptions and cancelations. In essence, paying your bills on time each month is essential for financial stability and overall well-being. If you pay your bills on time, you likely maintain a good credit score, which qualifies you for better financial products, lower interest rates, and more opportunities to flourish financially.

Believe it or not, I went through a phase in life where I was less than perfect with my finances. For a brief period in undergrad, paying my bills on time every month wasn't my top priority, and neither was consistently going to class if we're being honest. This phase lasted for about a year, and for one year, it seemed I was interested in everything else besides being a responsible adult. A year of wanting to have fun and "finding myself" turned into delinquent accounts and closed accounts, with some even going to collections. My credit score took a beating. It took me several years to fix just one year of irresponsible behavior! I can definitely say that I learned a lot from my mistakes, and there were plenty. Having poor finances was embarrassing, and it definitely made me feel less than confident about being in a relationship or even dating.

WHY THERE'S CONFLICT

The primary reason for conflict here is simple: not paying your bills on time. So, let's get into it! We know that financial difficulties can make it hard to pay bills on time and significantly contribute to conflict. But let's get a bit more nuanced and remove the assumption of financial hardship. The real meat of this topic is the behavior rather than the circumstance. While certain individuals don't pay their bills on time because they can't afford to, many don't because they forgot to or are straight up avoiding it. In a survey published by WalletHub in 2022 on late credit card payments, 45 percent of respondents cited the reason they didn't pay their bills on time was because they forgot and 7 percent cited they were too busy. (26)

The habit of not paying bills on time is a real problem that can cause frustration in a relationship. If a partner habitually misses payments, it shows a lack of responsibility and can present financial challenges that impact you and your partner. Forgetting to pay a bill can negatively impact your credit, creating a barrier to financial opportunities such as buying a home or automobile. The bottom line is if you or your partner aren't consistent with paying your bills on time, there is a higher likelihood that the relationship will suffer. The good news is we can fix this. You can implement steps to address the issues and reduce the chance of financial conflict.

DISCUSSION POINTS

The first step to reducing financial conflict and moving toward a path of financial compatibility is discussing the issues that lead to late or missed bill payments. It helps if one of you pay your bills on time as you will be responsible for leading the conversation with your partner and helping them better manage their bills. If both of you have a habit of not paying your bills on time, there's still hope for your relationship. Work together on the following discussion points, and make sure to note the steps you'll include in your *financial compatibility action plan.*

1. Discuss the consequences of not paying bills on time, such as late fees, a negative impact on credit scores, and increased financial stress.
2. Emphasize the benefits of paying bills on time, including maintaining a good credit score, avoiding additional charges, and achieving financial peace of mind.
3. Discuss setting up a system to manage bill payments, such as using automatic payments, setting calendar reminders, or designating specific days to review and pay bills.
4. Discuss incorporating bill payments into a monthly budget to ensure that funds are allocated appropriately.
5. Talk about organizing financial documents and bills to keep track of due dates and amounts owed. This could involve using folders, apps, or spreadsheets.
6. Encourage open communication about financial obligations and any challenges in meeting them. Regular discussions can help address potential issues before they become problems.
7. Discuss prioritizing essential expenses, such as housing, utilities, and car payments, to ensure they are paid on time before discretionary spending.
8. Discuss setting up a monthly check-in to ensure bills are paid timely.
9. Address any and all issues for missed payments and discuss ways to eliminate the issues.
10. Take this opportunity to evaluate all your outstanding bills and look at ways to reduce them if possible. There could be payments for unused streaming services or subscriptions that could be eliminated.

16

I BALANCE MY CHECKBOOK EVERY MONTH

Balancing your checkbook every month is ideal.
The preferred response is true.

WHY IT MATTERS

This topic is important for many reasons. But first, let's talk about the origin of the term "balance your checkbook." The language may be antiquated, but the meaning is still very relevant. Traditionally, this was an important task because you needed to do a reconciliation between the ledger in your checkbook, your record of the outstanding checks, and the monthly statement balance reported by your bank. This was necessary because the check-clearing process could take anywhere from several days to several weeks and may not have cleared before your statement was issued. Depending on how many checks you had outstanding, the difference between your bank statement balance and your ledger balance could be significant. Hence, the term "balance your checkbook." The term is now used to mean the process of reconciling your bank accounts. While we hardly use checkbooks anymore, the process of reconciling your bank accounts is still very important.

Balancing your bank accounts goes beyond reconciling outstanding checks. In today's world of electronic transactions, it's become much easier to complete transactions, and at the same time, it has become much easier to lose track of them. According to Tim

Maxwell, personal finance writer for Experian, you should reconcile your savings and checking account with your bank statements at least once every month. (27) Keeping track of all your transactions and knowing your exact balance helps you reduce the risk of overdrawing your account, which can result in costly overdraft fees or penalties. Reconciling your bank accounts goes even further. The process also offers a chance to review your spending habits. It helps you identify where your money is going, and it may highlight areas where you can save. It also helps you identify potentially fraudulent activity early on. In simple terms, reconciling your bank account is an essential tool for monitoring and managing your finances.

WHY THERE'S CONFLICT

Reconciling your bank accounts monthly is a valuable financial habit that promotes accuracy, accountability, and financial control. Adopting a habit of not monitoring your accounts can be very problematic. Losing track of your spending or accidentally overdrawing your account could lead to frustration and cause your partner to lose trust in your abilities to be financially responsible. This is another example of how irresponsible behavior can put a strain on your relationship. There tends to be an imbalance in your relationship where the more financially responsible partner ends up shouldering all the money-related responsibilities when one partner decides not to reconcile their bank accounts.

This unequal distribution of financial duties can make your relationship feel more like a parent-child relationship rather than that of equals in a partnership. The responsible partner may also become overwhelmed and exhausted from constantly having to monitor, track, and manage the household finances on their own, as they may worry about potential financial mistakes or oversights that their partner might make. This situation often results in decreased emotional intimacy since the responsible partner may consider the other partner unreliable or immature. The non-participating partner may also feel defensive and may even avoid talking about money altogether. This cycle can deteriorate the relationship's foundation in the long run, as financial teamwork is crucial for long-term stability and mutual respect.

My wife and I have very different ways of reconciling our accounts. I have a custom-made budgeting tool that allows me to upload all my transactions and to go through them line by line. My wife, on the other hand, reviews her transactions using the respective bank apps and checks for discrepancies. Surprisingly, as different as our approaches are, they both end with the same result. My wife keeps track of her accounts quite effectively, though I must admit initially, it was a point of conflict for us as I didn't think her way was enough. I slowly learned that there is more than one way to cook an egg, and in marriage, acknowledging that your wife is right comes with a few perks.

DISCUSSION POINTS

1. If applicable, start by discussing why you or your partner don't reconcile your bank accounts. Understanding the reasons why could help tailor the conversation.
2. Discuss the advantages of reconciling your bank accounts, such as catching errors or unauthorized transactions, avoiding overdraft fees, and gaining a clearer understanding of your financial standing.
3. Explore the availability of digital tools and apps that can simplify the process, making it less time-consuming and more convenient.
4. Emphasize how reconciling your bank accounts can help track spending habits, identify unnecessary expenses, and improve budgeting accuracy.
5. Discuss how regular reconciling can prevent overdrafts and the associated fees by ensuring there's always an accurate understanding of available funds.
6. Talk about the importance of sharing responsibilities and adopting a process that involves both you and your partner.
7. Suggest setting a regular schedule for reconciling your bank accounts, whether weekly or monthly, to make it a manageable and consistent habit.

8 Highlight how reconciling your bank accounts can build financial confidence and contribute to overall financial literacy.

17

I SET GOALS FOR THE THINGS I WANT TO PURCHASE

Having clear goals of the items you want to purchase is ideal. The preferred response is true.

WHY IT MATTERS

Here's what we already know from our previous discussion about the benefits of having clear goals for the items you purchase. It is known that setting purchase goals assists in making thoughtful spending decisions by focusing on what you really need and not spending money on nonessential things. Having specific goals is helpful in developing a plan for how to use your budgeted funds most effectively. In general, it is a good practice that supports good spending habits and sound financial management. The decision to make more conscious spending choices is one the most important things you can do for your financial stability. One thing I want to emphasize, and you probably won't read this in other books, is that having good spending habits does not mean that you should avoid spending. Don't get me wrong, if you don't need to spend money, then don't spend money. But you should spend money wisely to create or increase value. I'm not just talking about financial value; you should strive to achieve value in your livelihood, your well-being, and your financial outcomes.

WHY THERE'S CONFLICT

As mentioned, clear goals can help to eliminate impulse. Impulsive buying is a primary issue that can cause conflict in relationships. A recent study on impulse buying showed some alarming results. "Most shoppers (89 percent) have some history of impulse buying; 54 percent have spent $100 or more on an impulse buy." (28) This figure is especially alarming considering the negative impact that excessive impulse buying can have on your finances. Retailers take full advantage of the high propensity for impulse buying as some will strategically place items in the checkout aisle for this very reason. "Eighty percent of consumers shop impulsively in brick-and-mortar stores." (28) The old saying "I went into the store for a few things and came out with a cart" is a common reality. So then why is impulse buying a catalyst for conflict? It is for a number of reasons, primarily the implication of the habitual behavior of impulse buying. It's about self-control, or the lack thereof, that can ruin your finances and your relationship. This leads us to the next potential cause for conflict: emotional spending.

"Emotional spending is exactly what it sounds like. It's characterized by impulsive spending that's fueled by big emotions, such as stress, anxiety, or sadness." (29) This need to satisfy an emotional state with shopping is often the catalyst to compulsive shopping. Compulsive shopping is a real issue that could be classified as an addiction. If impulse shopping as a gateway drug, then compulsive shopping is the hardcore stuff. An interview by NerdWallet with Carrie Rattle, a financial therapist and coach, describes compulsive shoppers as follows: "If you're a compulsive shopper, it doesn't matter if there's a sale or if you already have that sweater in five colors. You shop to self-soothe." (30). She goes on to say that compulsive shoppers are extreme and may continue spending while they're in debt and harm relationships with their spending. (30) In fact, compulsive shopping behavior may be an indication of a more serious problem known as compulsive buying disorder. According to a study published in *World Psychiatry* by Dr. Donald Black, compulsive buying disorder (CBD) is characterized by excessive shopping cognitions and buying behavior that leads to distress or impairment. (31) He further states that CBD is a serious issue and is usually accompanied by other disorders particularly mood and anxiety disorders, substance use disorders, eating disorders, and other disorders of impulse control. (31) If you or your partner believes compulsive shopping might be an issue, then I encourage you to get the help that you need. Research support groups to join or seek out a professional who specializes in over shopping, such as a therapist, financial coach or clinical social worker. (30)

The next reason that could cause conflict when it comes to establishing goals for things you want to purchase is unincorporated purchases. Unincorporated purchases are purchases that are necessary but are not included in your budget. They are different from unplanned expenses, which come about due to unplanned circumstances. Rather, unincorporated purchases usually stem from poor budget planning. The unintended consequences of poor budgeting can be costly, and failing to include planned purchases ranks at the top of the list. It goes without saying that unincorporated purchases can be disruptive and could potentially trigger an argument. This is why it is so important to spend time reviewing your budget frequently to ensure that these types of mistakes aren't made, and if they are, they are caught promptly.

Defining specific purchase goals helps you better understand your financial situation, encouraging thoughtful decision-making about how much you can afford and when. But oftentimes, we make the decision to spend more than we planned on certain items. Overspending on planned items can be the cause of a lot of conflicts, especially when the decision to overspend is unilateral or made by one partner. Examples could be the decision to purchase a vehicle for forty thousand dollars, but instead, you spend forty-five thousand dollars. While this example is an obvious deviation from your spending goal, this issue more commonly manifests in smaller purchases, such as groceries and household items. These extra costs tend to accumulate and are more indicative of a pattern of overspending.

Overspending is a classic example of poor money management, which is the top reason why couples go over budget. Conflict often comes in the form of one partner asking the other why they spent so much on a particular item or why a particular bill is so high. Admittedly, I have been on the giving end of such inquiries into my wife's spending, and those conversations are never friendly. However, over the years, I've learned how to work with my wife to eliminate the need to ask about her spending habits and avoid conflict. Let's talk about the discussion points that you can leverage to help you avoid conflict.

DISCUSSION POINTS

1. Talk about the specific items you want to purchase and why these items are important. Understanding each other's motivations can help support each other's goals.
2. Discuss whether the desired items are needs or wants, and how they fit into your overall lifestyle and financial priorities.
3. Talk about how these items fit into your current budget, and whether adjustments are needed to accommodate these purchases without compromising other financial responsibilities.
4. Discuss ways to combine your efforts to control impulse spending. Is the ease of access to shopping online or via mobile apps making it easier to impulse shop?
5. Encourage researching the costs of the desired items and exploring any alternatives or deals. This can help in making informed decisions and potentially saving money.
6. Ensure that individual purchase goals align with any shared financial goals, such as saving for a vacation or paying off debt.

18

WHEN CHOOSING AN ITEM TO BUY, I SHOULD SELECT THE MOST EXPENSIVE OPTION IF I CAN AFFORD IT

Always going with the most expensive option even if you can afford it, is less than ideal. The preferred response is <u>false</u>.

WHY IT MATTERS

The most expensive option isn't always the best option, but neither is the cheapest option. This phrase pretty much sums up the reason why this topic is important. Higher priced items are intrinsically associated with higher quality. As consumers, we expect that if we're paying more for a product, then we are receiving more for our money. In fact, there are certain items that most consumers believe they should pay more for. A study conducted by Sickdeals, an online platform where community members rate the best deals on various products, found that two in three Americans state that some things are worth paying more for, provided they last longer, including cars, kitchen appliances, cookware, TVs, and phones. (32) The interesting thing to note here is that just the perception of the item lasting longer is enough for most people to choose the more expensive item. Even in the absence of information about a particular product, price is oftentimes held as a standard of quality.

So, what does all this mean? It sounds like the more expensive item may in fact yield the best quality and therefore the most value most of the time, right? Well, not so fast. This way of thinking is inherently flawed. Let's go back a step and talk about perceived value. "In marketing terminology, perceived value is a customer's evaluation of a product or a service's merits and its ability to meet their needs and expectations, especially compared with its peers. [...] Perceived value comes down to the price that the public is willing to pay for a good or service." (33) Herein lies the problem. According to an article by Valarie Zeithaml published in the *Journal of Marketing*, numerous studies have been done over several decades around the relationship with price and quality. "Despite the expectation of a positive relationship, results of these studies have provided mixed evidence." (34) The conclusion here is that price should not be the only determining factor of value. Furthermore, perceived value can be manipulated, and it often is. This is evident by the price disparity between luxury goods and other goods, despite the minimal difference in quality. "The highest value of luxury goods is associated not with their utility but with the prestige that owning and using it entails." (33) The reality is, what we know to be perceived value has been carefully curated by marketers to benefit the retailers and not the consumers.

WHY THERE'S CONFLICT

Regularly opting for the most expensive option can encourage materialistic habits and a reinforcement of the belief that a higher price equals greater happiness, which is often untrue. Mid-range or less expensive alternatives often offer comparable quality and utility without the premium price tag. Couples often have disagreements on how to go about selecting items to purchase. As noted, most people associate quality with price, so you are bound to have a few disagreements over which product to choose if you or your partner believe this to be true. Always choosing the most expensive option, even if you can afford it, can lead to overspending. It is also the primary reason for lifestyle inflation, where spending increases as your income grows. Premium-priced products are placed on a pedestal, and it's time we knock that pedestal down.

In today's world of readily available information and the ability to compare products easily, consumers have the ability to reshape how they determine value. The first step is to stop automatically holding the more expensive product as the gold standard to which we compare other products when making a purchasing decision. Instead, use more objective criteria for purchases and select the products that meet those criteria, regardless of price. Objective criteria, such as features, third-party product reviews, durability, standard warranties, customer support, etc., should be evaluated before considering the price. While price is certainly a factor in determining your purchase decision, it should not be the primary driving force of value. By adopting this rational spending approach to evaluating alternatives, you can make more deliberate decisions and ensure you get the best value for your money.

DISCUSSION POINTS

1 Discuss the relationship between cost and quality. Remember, while higher-priced items can sometimes offer better quality, it's not always the case.

2 Encourage evaluating products based on features, durability, and reviews rather than just price.

3 Emphasize the importance of value for money. Sometimes, mid-range or less expensive options provide similar benefits.

4 Talk about opportunity cost—the idea that spending more on certain items might reduce the ability to allocate funds toward other financial goals or experiences.

5 Discuss how choosing the most expensive options might impact your overall budget and shared financial goals, such as savings, investments, or future plans.

6 Discuss the need take a rational approach to spending by making purchasing decisions based on necessity and practicality rather than price or brand prestige.

19

I PAY MY ENTIRE CREDIT CARD STATEMENT BALANCES EACH MONTH

Paying your entire credit card statement balances each month is ideal. The preferred response is true.

WHY IT MATTERS

Paying your entire credit card statement balance each month is definitely the responsible thing to do, as it's a sure way to maintain financial stability and avoid unnecessary costs. Despite this, the majority of credit card users do not pay their entire balances each month. According to a recent survey by GOBankingRates, 56 percent of respondents stated that they did not pay their credit card bill in full each month. (35) This isn't likely due to a lack of knowledge of the consequences; if a person uses a credit card, then they've likely seen the disclaimers of only making the minimum payments. This is because the Credit Card Accountability Responsibility and Disclosure Act of 2009 (Credit CARD Act) required credit card companies to enhance their disclosures, which included enhanced disclosures on interest charges. (36) As a result, you now see in your credit card statement a summary of the amount of interest you would pay as well as the length of time to pay off the balance if you only made the minimum payment.

Making only the minimum payment on a credit card can take years to pay off a balance due to compounding interest. So, let's take a closer look and breakdown the details of that disclaimer that is presented in your credit card statements each month. Your disclaimer may look something similar to the table below. This is an example of how an actual minimum payment disclaimer would appear in most credit card statement, and most credit card companies are required to provide the same information.

If you make no additional charges and each month you pay...	You will pay off the balance shown on this statement in about...	And you will pay an estimated total of...
Only the Minimum Payment Due	18 years	$18,929
$274	3 years	$9,865 *(Savings = $9,064)*

The example shown here is for a statement balance of $7,113, with a minimum payment due of $142, or two percent of the statement balance. The interest rate is 22.49 percent, which is the typical interest rate on credit cards. By only paying the minimum payment, it would take 18 years to pay off the balance, and you would pay a whopping $11,816 in interest ($18,929 – $7,113). Increasing the monthly payment to $274 will pay off the balance in three years with only $2,752 in interest ($9,865 – 7,113). In either scenario, you fall victim to the trap of interest payments, and paying in full avoids this trap entirely.

Along with avoiding huge interest costs, there are other benefits that come with paying off your entire balance. Paying off your credit card in full helps maintain a low credit utilization. Your credit utilization is your outstanding balance as a percentage of your credit limit, and it is a key factor in determining your credit score. Utilization is calculated as follows:

$$\textit{Credit Utilization} = \frac{\text{Outstanding Balance}}{\text{Credit Limit}} \times 100$$

Let's use the same example as before and assume that the credit card has a limit of $20,000. With an outstanding balance of $7,113 and a credit card limit of $20,000, the utilization is approximately 36 percent. The generally accepted rule of thumb is to maintain a credit utilization of less than 30 percent in order to build and maintain a strong credit score.

WHY THERE'S CONFLICT

If you haven't already noticed, there is a pattern across the last five topics, so let me shed some light on this. If you and your partner scored differently, then there's a high likelihood that you will have some disagreements, and this is an indication of further conflict. It's what you should expect based on your compatibility matrix. Your objective is to find harmony one topic at a time. Now, in regards to your differences in approach to paying your credit card bills, there really is only one right approach, and you both must agree on that single approach. The bottom line is that carrying credit card balances month to month is an indication of improper debt management and poor spending habits, all of which are catalysts for problems within your relationship.

DISCUSSION POINTS

1. If applicable, start by understanding why you or your partner don't pay the full balance. Is it due to financial constraints, lack of awareness, or prioritization of other expenses?

2. Discuss how carrying a balance incurs interest and potentially late fees, which can increase the total amount owed and make it harder to pay off over time.

3. Discuss how consistently carrying a balance can affect your credit score, which is important for obtaining loans, mortgages, and even impacting insurance rates.

4. Discuss the importance of maintaining a low credit utilization ratio (the amount of credit used compared to the credit limit) to positively impact credit scores.

5 Talk about creating or adjusting your budget to prioritize paying down credit card balances. This might involve reallocating funds or cutting back on discretionary spending.

6 Explore strategies for paying off credit card debt, such as the snowball method (paying off the smallest balance first) or the avalanche method (focusing on the highest interest rate first).

7 Encourage avoiding new debt while working to pay down existing balances. This might involve using cash or a debit card for everyday purchases.

8 Discuss ways to prevent overspending, such as setting up spending alerts to notify you once you reach a self-determined spending threshold for the month.

20

CREDIT CARDS ARE FOR EMERGENCIES ONLY

The belief that credit cards should only be used for emergencies is less than ideal. The preferred response is false.

WHY IT MATTERS

This topic is a bit of a generational matter. As times have changed, so has the mindset around the use of credit cards. I mentioned in Topic 10 that growing up, my dad had a more traditional approach to credit card use and believed that they should only be used in emergencies when you don't have access to cash. He also believed in using his debit card in lieu of a credit card. His gospel at the time was to avoid using credit cards at all costs. He would always say: "If you don't have the cash to spend, then don't spend at all." Well, times have changed, and so has my dad.

Another important aspect of this topic that needs to be addressed is the idea that you keep a credit card around for emergencies instead of having an emergency fund. While a credit card can certainly be a source of liquidity during difficult circumstances, it is not an acceptable substitute for having an emergency fund.

What we know now about the convenience and value of using your credit cards has evolved. However, the old gospel from my dad still holds true: If you don't have the money to spend, then you shouldn't be spending at all. There are several benefits to responsible use of credit cards. But first, let me say this. There are no benefits from using your debit card to make purchases. As a matter of fact, it is more likely that you will put yourself at an increased risk of fraud by using your debit card to make purchases. I highly recommend that you replace your everyday debit card use with a credit card, and only use your debit card to make cash withdrawals. Now, let's talk more about why using a credit card for all your normal purchases is a more practical approach.

Using a credit card for day-to-day purchases provides a number of benefits. First, credit cards can help you manage your cash flow for regular purchases, such as groceries or gas, allowing you to make payments at the end of the billing cycle and reducing the need for day-to-day reconciling. Credit cards often come with rewards, such as cash back, travel points, and even discounts. If you only use your credit card for emergencies, you forgo the chance to earn these rewards on everyday purchases. Credit cards offer protections like travel insurance, purchase protection, or extended warranties, oftentimes at no additional cost to you. Credit cards also offer strong fraud protection and safeguards against unauthorized charges, which is much safer than using your debit card. By using credit cards for everyday purchases instead of just emergencies, you can take advantage of all these benefits compared to using debit cards or cash.

WHY THERE'S CONFLICT

Responsible and regular credit card use should be a tool that works for you and not just a last resort during emergencies. It should be part of your arsenal of healthy financial habits. However, credit card use does have its downside, specifically when it comes to excess use. Overusing credit can be problematic. Excess use of credit cards is usually a symptom of bigger issues when it comes to financial mismanagement. Signs of credit overuse include constant credit card balances, maxed-out credit cards, late or missed payments, increasing debt load, minimum payments, and denied credit applications. (37) Credit overuse has big implications on the stability of your relationship as it shifts the focus away from your financial goals to addressing poor spending habits, not to mention the negative impact on your credit, limiting your ability to qualify for financial products.

On the flip side, you could find yourself in a disagreement with your partner due to a lack of credit use. This is an interesting dynamic, as the lack of credit use does pose its share of issues. The lack of credit use, or the lack of credit in general, also presents the issue of not being able to qualify for financial products, like a mortgage when the time comes. Imagine finding out that your partner has no credit history when house hunting. This revelation presents a hurdle that could set you back from achieving a life-long goal. Your partner may have been under the impression that staying away from credit use was the right approach, working hard to avoid the perceived traps and pitfalls of credit card use. This now puts you in the situation of reevaluating your life-long dream and having an uncomfortable conversation with your partner. Given this scenario, I'm actually not sure which conversation is worse: the conversation with a partner with bad credit from overuse or the one with a partner with no credit at all. What are your thoughts on this?

DISCUSSION POINTS

1. Discuss the benefits of using credit cards responsibly, such as earning rewards, cash back, or travel points.
2. Discuss any apprehension you or your partner may have about using credit. What caused your fear of credit?
3. Talk about ways to overcome your apprehension of using credit, like taking small steps, such as purchasing small items with a credit card and paying them off immediately.
4. Discuss how regular, responsible use of a credit card can help build a strong credit history.
5. Talk about the added benefit of better fraud protection compared to debit cards, making credit cards a safer option for online purchases.

6 Talk about concerns about debt by emphasizing the importance of paying the balance in full each month to avoid interest charges and debt accumulation.

7 Discuss strategies for managing credit responsibly, such as setting spending limits and automatic payments.

21

A CREDIT CARD CAN BE A VALUABLE TOOL TO IMPROVE YOUR FINANCES

The belief that a credit card can be a valuable tool to improve your finances is ideal. The preferred response is true.

WHY IT MATTERS

In Topic 20, we talked about the various benefits of using a credit card for day-to-day purchases. Credit cards offer the ability to manage your cash flow for regular purchases, allowing you to make payments at the end of the billing cycle and reducing the need for day-to-day reconciling. Credit cards offer rewards, such as cash-back, travel points, and even discounts. Credit cards offer protections like travel insurance, purchase protection, or extended warranties, oftentimes at no additional cost to you. Credit cards also offer strong fraud protection and safeguards against unauthorized charges. But while these benefits provide some improvements to your finances, there are more salient benefits that credit cards can provide that can have a positive impact on your finances.

Many of the benefits listed apply to individuals who have well-established credit and qualify for cards that offer these amazing benefits. What about individuals with no credit who can't qualify for these high-end cards? We previously discussed the need to establish credit, and how the lack of credit can inhibit you from acquiring lending products. A credit card can provide one of the easiest paths to establishing a credit history. According to NerdWallet, options for your first credit card include secured cards, store cards, student cards, and alternative cards, as well as finding a co-signer or becoming an authorized user on someone else's account. (38) Using your card to make small purchases and paying your balance in full each month is a safe way to build your credit in as little as six months. A credit card can also be a useful tool to help rebuild credit. Again, the key to maximizing the benefits is through responsible use, paying balances in full and on time, and avoiding overspending. This will ensure that the card works for your financial goals rather than against them. When used wisely, a credit card is more than just a payment method; it is a financial tool that can help build credit, improve money management skills, and provide access to other lending products.

Credit cards can also be a tool to improve the finances of even more veteran users with well-established credit. We mentioned that one of the benefits was the ability to manage your cash flow for regular purchases, allowing you to make payments at the end of the billing cycle. This may seem like more of a convenience benefit. However, there is a tangible financial outcome that we can achieve here, and many savvy individuals take advantage of the strategy of maximizing earning potential on an interest-bearing account. The key to this strategy is to maximize the average daily balance used to calculate interest each month by using a credit card for daily transactions in combination with an interest-bearing account. To better illustrate this, let's consider the following example: You get paid bi-weekly (every two weeks), and your net pay is $2,500. You currently have a checking account where you use your debit card to make transactions throughout the month that total $2,000. Your current checking account does not earn interest. So, how can we take advantage of a strategy that earns interest?

There are two things that need to happen. First, you need to open a high-yield checking account (HYCA), and use it instead of your regular checking account. Have your paycheck directly deposited into your HYCA, and link your credit card to your HYCA to automatically pay your balance on the due date. Credit card payment due dates are typically 10 to 15 days after the monthly billing cycle. Let's assume you open the HYCA on January 1st with a balance of \$2,500. The annual percentage yield (APY) on the HYCA is 0.5 percent. The following table is an illustration of your monthly average daily balance and interest earned using your old checking account and debit card (Balance 1) against your monthly average daily balance (Balance 2) and interest earned using your HYCA and credit card.

Month	Balance 1	Interest 1	Balance 2	Interest 2
January	\$3,894	\$0	\$4,919	\$2
February	\$7,259	\$0	\$9,181	\$4
March	\$10,382	\$0	\$12,312	\$5
April	\$13,849	\$0	\$15,778	\$6
May	\$17,360	\$0	\$19,292	\$8
June	\$20,862	\$0	\$22,792	\$9
July	\$24,263	\$0	\$26,196	\$11
August	\$27,757	\$0	\$29,691	\$13
September	\$31,226	\$0	\$33,159	\$14
October	\$34,733	\$0	\$36,604	\$16
November	\$38,254	\$0	\$40,188	\$17
December	\$41,667	\$0	\$43,604	\$19
Annual Total		**\$0**		**\$123**

This illustration demonstrates the tangible benefit of using a credit card and how it can improve your financial outcome. Notice that the balance used to calculate interest is larger when using a credit card as you carry forward your monthly expenses. You are essentially receiving an interest-free loan for one month. While the outcome seems relatively small, the benefit of holding your cash for a longer period in an account that earns interest is still relevant.

Another way credit cards could improve your finances is through debt consolidation. Oftentimes, credit cards offer the opportunity to transfer balances with a low APR, as low as zero percent, for a duration of time, typically 12 to 18 months. This could be part of a strategy to reduce high-interest debt. Keep in mind there are upfront fees that are typically 3 to 5 percent of the amount transferred. You may have to apply for a new credit card unless an offer exists on a card you already own. Despite the upfront fee, this could be a useful way to pay off debt and minimize high interest costs. Using this strategy requires you to have discipline above and beyond the circumstances that required you to reduce your debt in the first place.

WHY THERE'S CONFLICT

We previously discussed how conflict can occur from having different approaches to using credit. Overusing and not using credit at all can negatively impact your finances and create turmoil within your relationship. A difference in beliefs in the useful nature of credit cards could be the cause of conflict. You or your partner may see credit cards as risky and unnecessary because of the potential to accumulate debt, high interest rates, and the temptation to overspend. You or your partner may choose to avoid debt entirely, even at the cost of not being able to establish and build credit. Finding common ground and adopting a philosophy that utilizes credit cards to improve your finances and, at the same time, makes everyone feel comfortable in the process is key to avoiding conflict.

DISCUSSION POINTS

1. Share each other's perspective and why each of you feels the way you do about credit cards.
2. If applicable, discuss possible reasons for skepticism about credit cards. Have you or your partner had negative experiences or concerns about credit card use?
3. Talk about how using a credit card responsibly can help build a good credit history, which is essential for obtaining loans, mortgages, and even some job opportunities.

4 Explore how paying the full balance each month allows the use of interest-free periods, effectively borrowing money without incurring additional costs.

5 Talk about strategies for responsible credit card use, such as setting spending limits, paying balances in full, and avoiding impulse purchases.

6 Discuss other ways you can leverage credit cards to improve your finances, such as zero-interest financing and debt consolidation.

22

I WOULD TAKE ON MORE DEBT THAN PLANNED TO BUY MY FOREVER HOME

Taking on more debt than planned to buy your forever home is less than ideal. The preferred response is false.

WHY IT MATTERS

This topic might ruffle a few feathers because it's a topic that many feel passionate about. Achieving the dream of homeownership is exciting—especially when it's your forever home. But if the price is outside your comfort zone, it may require significant lifestyle changes to afford the mortgage. This kind of rationalizing can lead to taking on more debt than planned, which is risky. Overspending on a home can strain your finances, limit your ability to meet other goals, and ultimately reduce your quality of life. The term "house poor" comes to mind. When you take on too big of a mortgage, it becomes a burden to cover essential expenses, like groceries and everyday living.

Homeownership also comes with additional costs that you need to factor into your budget, such as home furnishings and appliances, maintenance and repairs, utilities, home improvements, pest control, and home security. (3) A larger mortgage payment can also create a more stressful environment as you live in constant fear of what will happen should your economic circumstances change. In addition, having all your income going towards this monster of a mortgage makes handling unforeseen costs like medical bills or home repairs difficult. If the housing market declines and you owe more on your mortgage than the house is worth, selling or refinancing can become challenging. So, let's take a closer look at mortgage affordability.

When it comes to affordability, most lending experts say that your mortgage payment should be no more than 30 percent of your monthly income. However, more people are finding that may not cut it. Home prices have gone up along with interest rates in recent years, and more people are exceeding that 30 percent mark. According to an NBC News analysis of Census Bureau data, 30 percent of middle-class homeowners bought homes with mortgage payments that exceeded 30 percent of their income. (39) More people are overextending themselves in order to purchase a home and putting themselves at an increased risk of financial hardship in the process.

WHY THERE'S CONFLICT

Finding your forever home should not come down to deciding between your dream and being financially prudent. Conflicts can emerge when you and your partner are on opposing ends of that decision. Usually, one partner may feel more comfortable overextending themselves and strongly believes the means justify the end if it means getting their forever home. Approach this discussion gently, as emotions tend to flare when dreams are involved. For them, it feels like they've been working so long to achieve this goal, and now that it's within reach, you're trying to ruin it by saying, "We can't afford it."

This topic is especially relatable to me, as my wife always says that her dream is to have a house with a pool. We currently don't have a pool, and she makes it a point to remind me of that when she shows me listings of homes with pools for sale in our neighborhood. We've had a number of discussions where I've said it's simply not a wise decision, and for the most part, she does understand. But that doesn't stop her from forwarding those listings. Despite my reservations about buying a new house with a pool, I still have to acknowledge my wife's desires, and incorporating them as part of our shared goals is important. What that says to her is that even though we can't afford to get the house with the pool now, it doesn't mean we won't get it later as we work toward achieving our goals.

DISCUSSION POINTS

1. Discuss the long-term financial impact of taking on more debt, including higher monthly payments, interest costs, and the potential strain on your budget and other financial goals.

2. Talk about what you can comfortably afford while maintaining your lifestyle and financial stability.

3. Talk about the importance of avoiding becoming "house poor," where a larger portion of income goes to housing expenses, leaving you little to spend on other essentials.

4. Discuss the potential stress and impact on your relationship that the increased financial burden can bring.

5. Explore how interest rates and loan terms affect the total cost of the home and monthly payments. A larger loan might have significant financial implications over time.

6. Discuss current real estate market conditions and whether it's a favorable time to buy. Sometimes, waiting can result in better opportunities or a more favorable mortgage.

23

I SHOULD CONTROL THE MONEY IN THE MARRIAGE

Control of the money by one individual in a relationship is less than ideal. The preferred response is <u>false</u>.

WHY IT MATTERS

In a marriage, effective financial management is essential for the well-being and stability of the partnership. While it might seem efficient for one partner to handle all the financial matters, this can lead to some disadvantages that can impact the relationship. Having some level of shared responsibility is ideal. "How you determine financial responsibilities can be challenging, but it's essential to building a solid foundation for your future together." (3) In *Marriage & Finances*, I discuss the importance of incorporating a plan that includes a division of financial responsibilities. I established a three-step method to managing responsibilities as a team.

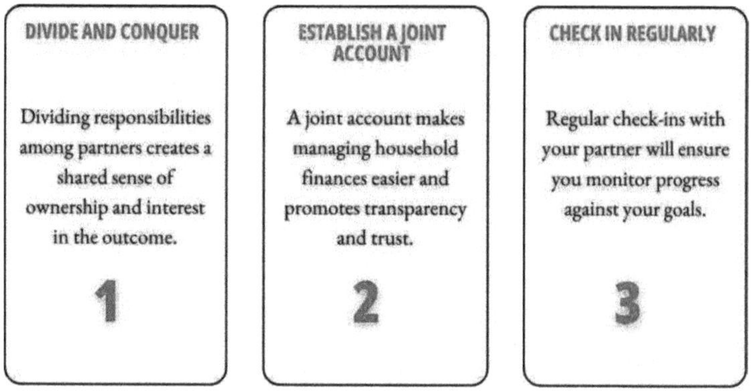

This three-step approach enhances your ability to reach your financial goals while maintaining relationship harmony.

Step 1 – Divide and conquer
Step 2 – Establish a joint account
Step 3 – Check in regularly

The first step involves establishing who will take care of what. "Dividing financial responsibilities promotes a sense of shared responsibility for the well-being of the household. Both partners work together to achieve shared financial goals and feel greater ownership over the household's financial situation." (3) The process of dividing responsibilities doesn't have to be detailed and cumbersome. Still, it should be formal enough that each partner knows what they're responsible for each month without the need to be reminded of tier responsibilities. First, start by clearly identifying all the various responsibilities, from organizing the grocery shopping to reconciling the bank accounts. Each partner should take ownership of their tasks and take comfort in knowing that the other tasks are being handled by their partner.

Couples should divide their responsibilities, regardless of who makes more income. Income should not be a determining factor for who gets to control the money in the marriage. You should understand that even if you are the sole income contributor, it does not diminish the role that your partner has and the value they bring to the marriage. As we discussed in Topic 5, choosing whether to have a single or dual-income household comes down to the decision that makes the most sense for your household. Hence, being the sole income contributor does not give you the right to diminish your partner's contribution because the arrangement was a joint decision.

WHY THERE'S CONFLICT

Having one person in the relationship control the finances is an inherent recipe for conflict. When one person makes all the financial decisions, it eliminates the relationship benefits that come from collaboration and teamwork. It is true what they say: Two minds are better than one, especially when it comes to life-changing decisions around finance and money management. Having both of you contribute toward financial management makes sure that there are different ideas that are helpful in forming better decisions and financial strategies. It also helps maintain trust and transparency and avoids confusion.

Another drawback of vesting all the power to make financial decisions with one partner is that the other partner has a high level of dependency and is not involved at all. This lack of involvement means that the other partner misses the opportunity of a chance to build on their financial literacy skills, which could be dangerous as this leaves them financially unprepared in the event of an illness or death.

DISCUSSION POINTS

Involving both partners in money matters brings equality, improves communication, and benefits your relationship. The relationship thrives on both partners feeling empowered and informed of their financial situation and working together as a team to meet their shared goals.

1. If applicable, start by understanding why you or your partner feels one person should control the finances. Knowing their reasoning can help guide the discussion.

2. Talk. about the benefits of both partners being involved in financial decisions, including promoting transparency, accountability, and mutual understanding of your financial situation.

3. Discuss how joint financial management ensures that both partners' goals and values are represented in financial decisions, fostering a sense of partnership and collaboration.

4. Talk about how shared financial management can build trust and improve communication, helping to prevent misunderstandings or conflicts related to money.

5. Discuss any concerns or fears either partner might have about shared financial management and work together to address these issues constructively.

6. Discuss how you will divide and conquer. Look at ways to divide responsibilities based on strengths or your desire to take on certain tasks.

7. Talk about how you can consolidate and manage your finances by using a joint account.

8. Schedule a recurring time to meet to review and discuss your finances. You should meet at least once per month.

24

I BELIEVE IT IS IMPORTANT TO SAVE

Saving for the future is definitely ideal. The preferred response is true.

WHY IT MATTERS

There is broad consensus that it is important to save However, not everyone actually practices what they preach. Saving levels are at a record low. A recent study of bank account balances by GO-BankingRates found that half of Americans have less than $500 in savings, with 36 percent having $100 or less in savings. (40) This is far from ideal and is not sufficient to cover unforeseen expenses or emergencies.

When it comes to retirement savings accounts, the story is a bit of a mixed bag. Most American workers feel that they will have enough to live comfortably upon retirement. However, this positive outlook may be partly because of the reliance of employer pensions and government social security that they feel are guaranteed and less from personal contributions into retirement savings accounts. "As of late 2023, workers have saved $64,000 (estimated median) in total household retirement accounts." (41) This is far from the $1.5 million needed to live on by most estimates.

The primary reason for personal savings is the financial security it provides. Unexpected challenges can occur at any time, and a financial cushion allows you to navigate these situations without resorting to debt. Saving is also important for long-term goals, such as buying a home. Savings play a significant role in retirement planning, which is another critical area. Because traditional social security and pension plans are dwindling, individuals, now more than ever, have had to take responsibility for their retirement. It is possible to ensure you have adequate retirement funding through early planning and consistent saving. Hence, it's important for you to establish a savings plan. Your savings plan involves setting financial targets and developing a strategy to achieve them. (3) Your savings plan can be accomplished by following these four steps:

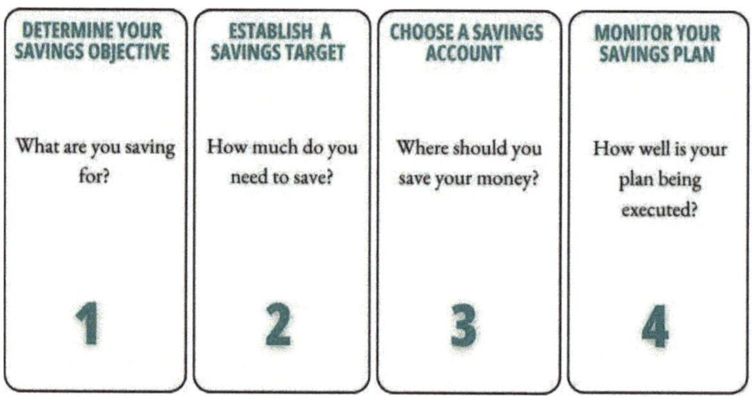

Committing to saving encourages you to evaluate your spending habits, helping you to avoid unnecessary debt and securing your financial future.

WHY THERE'S CONFLICT

Despite the known benefits, couples often deprioritize savings for various reasons. Primary reasons include living above their means and overspending on lifestyle and experiences. Deprioritizing savings can be problematic when circumstances change for the worse, and having those savings could have been the necessary lifeline. Deprioritizing savings also jeopardizes your ability to achieve your goals, financial or otherwise. Your relationship is put to the ultimate test when problems and circumstances occur that could have been avoided had you made better choices and placed more emphasis on savings. Your ability to successfully navigate your relationship involves making decisions that benefit you in the long run. Choosing to forego savings for short-lived experiences or lifestyle upgrades puts your finances and your relationship at risk.

Another major cause of conflict is the mishandling of savings by one partner. We've all seen the movie where a person loses their life savings in pursuit of a fruitless dream or squanders their savings on a frivolous purchase, putting the livelihood of the family at risk because of their poor judgment. These scenarios are very real, and we see real lives impacted because of one person's willful actions. In the legal world, this is called marital waste, and it's a leading cause of divorce. "Marital waste is when one spouse spends community money or community assets irresponsibly or for their sole benefit." (42) One person's willingness to be cavalier with savings that took years and dedication to amass would definitely be grounds for reconsidering the relationship if they can so carelessly throw it all away. There is a saying, "Money isn't everything," but when do you draw the line?

Finally, a more fundamental cause for conflict in terms of savings is when you and your partner have a misalignment or disagreement on savings goals. You may want to prioritize saving for retirement and allocate as many funds to that goal as possible, while your partner may want to place more emphasis on purchasing a home and allocate funds differently to accommodate that goal. This really comes down to how you prioritize and quantify your shared financial goals. "Establishing financial goals provides focus and helps prioritize spending and saving decisions." (3) Establishing financial goals that both partners agree on is your one sure way of minimizing disagreements and avoiding conflicts down the road. I highly recommend adopting the SMART method when establishing and documenting your goals. "The SMART goal-setting approach is a widely recognized framework that helps you set and achieve your objectives effectively. SMART stands for Specific, Measurable, Achievable, Realistic, and Timely." (3)

Let's look at an example of how you would use the SMART method to document the objective of saving for a down payment on a home to achieve the goal of homeownership.

Specific	Save for a five percent down payment on a home in the price range of $400,000.
Measurable	Save monthly or bi-weekly, for a total of $20,000.
Achievable	Save $1,667 monthly, or $769 bi-weekly, by cutting back on expenses and reprioritizing our savings temporarily toward this objective.
Realistic	A five percent down payment is required to qualify for a specific loan program. The loan program is a feasible path to achieving our dream of home ownership.
Timely	Achieve the objective in 12 months, or 26 weeks.

DISCUSSION POINTS

1 If you haven't done so already, now is the time to establish shared financial goals. Use the SMART method to document your goals.

2 Talk about how saving can help you achieve shared financial goals, such as buying a home, traveling, or starting a family.

3 Discuss the importance of saving for retirement to ensure financial independence and security in later years.

4 Discuss how having a savings cushion or an emergency fund can reduce anxiety about money, providing peace of mind knowing you're prepared for life's uncertainties.

5 Discuss how saving encourages better financial habits, such as budgeting and mindful spending, which contribute to long-term financial health.

6 Talk about the importance of prioritizing savings over non-essential expenses. This might involve making lifestyle adjustments to free up more money for your emergency fund

7 Discuss starting with a small, manageable amount and gradually increasing your savings over time.

8 Discuss the type of account to use, such as a high yield savings account (HYSA) to help maximize savings.

25

I SHOULD BE ABLE TO PUT MONEY AWAY AND NOT TELL MY PARTNER

Putting money away and not telling your partner is definitely not ideal. The preferred response is <u>false</u>.

WHY IT MATTERS

In a relationship, particularly in marriage or long-term partnerships, trust and transparency are very important, especially when it comes to finances. Keeping financial matters secret, like having undisclosed savings accounts, can undermine this trust and lead to conflict in your relationship. This type of behavior falls under the umbrella of a concept known as financial infidelity. A study published in the *Journal of Consumer Research* defines financial infidelity as engaging in any financial behavior expected to be disapproved of by one's romantic partner and intentionally failing to disclose this behavior to them. (43) The authors of the study go on to state that both the disapproving financial behavior and the act of concealment are what qualifies as financial infidelity. (43) Financial infidelity is quite common. A recent poll by Bankrate of individuals in committed relationships revealed that 40 percent of respondents admitted to committing actions that would be considered financial infidelity. (44) A closer look at the actions reveals that 33 percent admitted to spending more than their partner would be okay with, 23 percent admitted to holding secret debt, and 15 percent admitted to having a secret savings account. (44)

The act of putting money away and hiding it from your partner certainly qualifies as financial infidelity. Full disclosure of your financial situation is an essential part of any long-term relationship. This includes disclosing all assets, including bank accounts. Failure to disclose these assets and other aspects of your finances shows a lack of financial intimacy with your partner. "Financial intimacy is the level of openness and communication between partners regarding their finances. It involves sharing financial information and making joint decisions about money matters." (3) Being open and honest about your finances reinforces your commitment to each other and promotes a healthier and stronger relationship.

WHY THERE'S CONFLICT

The need to hide money from your partner may point to deeper issues in the relationship. Discovering financial secrets can lead to conflict and raise concerns about what else your partner might be hiding. It can plant seeds of distrust and even feelings of betrayal. The very nature of financial infidelity is an automatic prerequisite for conflict. It's only a matter of time before your partner discovers your secret. But what if you never intended it to be a secret? What if you genuinely believe that it is important to maintain a level of financial independence and that it's perfectly fine to save money on the side and not disclose it to your partner?

There are some of you whose response to this topic is rooted in the belief that you should maintain a level of financial independence. For the most part, you absolutely should. In fact, having a level of financial independence is healthy. Financial independence may look like having your own account, separate from any joint accounts. You may have your own credit cards and even investment accounts—and that's perfectly fine. What's not okay is keeping these accounts hidden from your partner. Remember, the components of financial infidelity are twofold: disapproving behavior and concealment. Suppose you and your partner agree to have separate accounts and disclose them. In that case, this is perfectly acceptable and even beneficial to the relationship.

DISCUSSION POINTS

1. Discuss how financial secrecy can impact trust and lead to misunderstandings or feelings of betrayal.

2. If applicable, ask your partner about their reasons for wanting to save money privately. Understanding their motivations can help address underlying concerns or fears they may have about finances.

3. Discuss ways to ensure both partners feel secure and independent financially, such as having individual accounts for personal spending alongside joint accounts for shared expenses.

4. Work together to find a compromise that respects both partners' needs and preferences. This could involve a system where both partners have discretionary funds or agree on individual savings goals.

5. Discuss ways to strengthen your partnership through collaborative financial planning, completely eliminating the need for financial secrecy.

26

I WOULD NEVER CONSIDER OPENING A JOINT ACCOUNT

Not having some form of joint account with your partner is not ideal. The preferred response is false.

WHY IT MATTERS

In Topic 23, we discussed the importance of managing financial responsibilities and using a three-step method to accomplish this.

Step 1 – Divide and conquer
Step 2 – Establish a joint account
Step 3 – Check in regularly

The second step to effectively managing financial responsibilities involves providing a means to facilitate transparency and centralize operations using a joint account. Evidence shows there is a strong correlation between having a joint account and having a successful relationship. A recent study in the *Journal of Personality and Social Psychology* concluded that couples who pool all their finances experience greater relationship satisfaction and are less likely to break up compared to couples who keep some or all of their finances separate. (45) Establishing a joint account could even reduce the likelihood of financial infidelity. I should note that while creating a system to facilitate greater transparency may reduce the likelihood of financial infidelity, it does not prevent it. So, let's talk about all the other ways you can benefit from having a joint account.

Having a joint account provides a number of benefits that enhance both your ability to manage your finances and the quality of your relationship. A recent study published in the *Journal of Consumer Research* states that joint accounts are especially beneficial for newlyweds. The study led by Jenni Olson, a marketing professor at Indiana University, showed that couples who merge their money in a joint account sustained strong relationship quality throughout the first two years of marriage over those who kept separate accounts. (46) The study showed that, contrary to the typical decline in relationship satisfaction often seen in the early years of marriage, combining finances not only prevented that decline but actually increased satisfaction. (46) These findings are eye-opening in showing the key relationship benefits of having a joint account. It shows that merging finances improves how partners feel about how they handle money, promotes alignment on financial goals, and sustains adherence to communal norms. (46) Communal norms are observed when partners in a relationship do things for each other without expectations of reciprocity.

For me, having a joint account has helped us maintain transparency as it ensures that both my wife and I have access to the income, expenses, and savings information. A joint account has been especially useful in managing household expenses. We utilize a joint credit card to manage and track all of our household expenses, and we make monthly payments with a joint checking account. Our approach makes things simpler by centralizing transactions and reducing complexity. It also promotes accountability, as it is easier to track spending patterns and tweak your budgets accordingly.

WHY THERE'S CONFLICT

Not merging your finances and keeping them separate has been shown to increase the chance of conflict in your relationship. As previously mentioned, studies have shown that not merging your finances can increase the likelihood of financial infidelity and reduce relationship satisfaction. However, despite this, more and more of the younger generation is opting to have separate accounts.

A survey done by Bankrate revealed; "45 percent of younger millennials, ages 26 to 32, who are married, in a civil partnership or living with their partner don't share any accounts, compared to 20 percent of Gen Xers and 14 percent of baby boomers." (47) This is in line with a growing trend for an increased need for financial autonomy and independence amongst couples.

This growing need to maintain financial independence tends to cause conflict between those who want total autonomy and those who want a complete merger. In Topic 25, we talked about why it is healthy to maintain a level of financial independence. However, complete autonomy runs the risk of not working as a team to manage one of the most important aspects of your relationship: your financial future. Therefore, I firmly believe that you can maintain your independence and still take advantage of the benefits of having a joint account.

My wife and I kept our individual checking accounts, which we had before getting married. We each have access to each other's personal accounts, but we manage all of our household expenses through our joint account. I guess you can say we have the best of both worlds, where even though we've merged our finances, we still have the independence that comes from maintaining our own accounts, which are fully transparent, of course.

DISCUSSION POINTS

1. If applicable, talk about your reasons for not wanting to merge your finances and open a joint account. What are your concerns?

2. Review the benefits of having a joint account, which we discussed in this topic. Are there any additional benefits you can achieve?

3. Explore potential compromises, such as starting with a joint account for specific purposes like household bills or vacation savings, to ease into the idea gradually.

4. Talk about your shared financial goals and how a joint account could facilitate achieving these goals by streamlining savings and spending.

5 Discuss the importance of ensuring both partners are informed and involved in financial decisions.

6 Reassure your partner that opening a joint account doesn't mean giving up financial autonomy. Talk about how you can both maintain individual accounts for personal spending while using the joint account for shared expenses. This setup supports both independence and collaboration.

27

I WOULD NOT LIKE IT IF MY PARTNER MADE MORE MONEY THAN ME

Having the sentiment of not wanting your partner to make more money than you is not ideal. The preferred response is false.

WHY IT MATTERS

So far, we've talked about several topics that, to some, could be considered controversial in the sense that the topics cause a bit of discourse and debate. This is one of those topics. However, in order to truly understand why this topic is controversial, we first need to understand the background and why income disparities between partners might be problematic. Traditional sentiments of the larger income earner being tied to the head of the household are ingrained into our culture. Being the "breadwinner" has always been thought to be the person who goes out and makes sure the family is able to have a roof over their heads and food on the table. This is just some of the language I heard growing up, and believe it or not, it is still pretty much the same today. Income is intrinsically tied to the ability to provide and to a person's sense of worth. This sense of worth is often tied to the masculine role in a heterosexual relationship dynamic. "Roughly seven in ten adults (71 percent) say it is very important for a man to be able to support a family financially to be a good husband or partner." (48) This sentiment still exists even though we are seeing more women become substantial income earners. This aspect of income tied to the man in the relationship has dominated our society, as this so-called "masculine role" is ubiquitous across other relationship dynamics (same sex) as well. However, research shows that the issue of income differences between partners is more problematic amongst heterosexual couples than it is with same-sex couples. Same-sex couples prioritize equitable earnings and demonstrate more progressive gender views compared to heterosexual couples. (49) So, it would seem that income differences between partners have been and continue to be an issue for heterosexual couples, particularly when the man makes less than the woman.

WHY THERE'S CONFLICT

Income differences between heterosexual partners are a common occurrence. In heterosexual couples, men often place a higher emphasis on being financial providers. In approximately two-thirds of married or cohabiting couples, men earn more than women. (48) However, as more women become substantial income earners, we see more instances where women are the primary income earners. This presents a dilemma in some relationships as the attachment to the traditional sentiment that the man should make more money still exists. Conflicts can arise if one or both partners have traditional sentiments about income and the role it plays in determining gender norms, specifically as it pertains to the masculine role. Feeling uncomfortable when your partner earns more can lead to resentment as opposed to a sense of pride and accomplishment for your partner.

Focusing on income differences can negatively impact your relationship, shifting the focus from a harmonious partnership to a disruptive competition. This shift in focus can create an unhealthy power dynamic where one partner feels superior or inferior, affecting the overall relationship satisfaction. Men tend to avoid talking about their feelings about the matter, partly for fear they may come off as chauvinistic for feeling the way they do. And perhaps there may be some of those tendencies buried deep down, but that's for another book to solve. For now, it's important to have open, honest conversations with your partner to challenge outdated beliefs about gender roles and income. Since money is a common source of tension in relationships, avoiding these discussions can lead to greater conflict. Additionally, tying self-worth to income can harm self-esteem and make it harder to recognize the value of non-financial contributions to the relationship.

I recall having a spirited debate with a good friend of mine about this topic. He argued that in no circumstance should his significant other make more than him. His reasoning was that if his partner were to make more than him, then that would change the dynamics of the relationship. He said that his wife would now "wear the pants in the relationship," and that would inhibit her ability to be a good mother to their children. His way of thinking was completely rooted in the belief that income is directly tied to the value of one's contribution to the relationship. I posed several questions.

First, I asked, "At what point does the difference in income become irrelevant? If you made one million dollars and your partner made two million dollars, would it matter that she made more? Also, why would she focus less on your children if she made more money than you?" Lastly, I asked him, "Would it mean that you would be more involved in raising your children in order for your partner to pursue her career goals. Would that make you less of a man?" His answers pretty much confirmed his traditional views, and even though I completely disagreed with his perspective, I listened and I didn't judge. I realize that some of you may share my friend's perspective, and to that end, I say, "Remember the pledge you made at the beginning of this journey."

DISCUSSION POINTS

1. If applicable, share your feelings and concerns about the income disparity. Understanding each other's perspective can help address any underlying issues.

2. Emphasize that a relationship is a partnership, and both partners' contributions, whether financial or otherwise, are valuable and important.

3 Discuss how societal norms and expectations might influence feelings about income and identity. Encourage an open conversation about how these perceptions affect your relationship.

4 Talk about the importance of self-worth and identity beyond financial earnings. Encourage each other to recognize and appreciate the diverse contributions each partner brings to the relationship.

5 Discuss how celebrating each other's achievements can strengthen your bond and create a more supportive partnership.

28

I SHOULD BE ABLE TO LEND MONEY TO A RELATIVE WITHOUT FIRST SPEAKING WITH MY PARTNER

Lending money to a relative without first speaking with my partner is not ideal. The preferred response is false.

WHY IT MATTERS

Before we dive into this topic, let me address something you may have wondered when you were marking your response. You may have thought that more context is needed around the threshold of money that requires partner approval. Well, just in case you were wondering, I worded the topic without any context for a reason. On one hand, you could be lending a relative twenty dollars for parking. On the other hand, you could be loaning or investing twenty thousand dollars to a relative to start a business. I think we can all agree that we wouldn't necessarily call our partner about the twenty-dollar loan. However, most of us would have a conversation with our partner about the investment opportunity before committing to twenty thousand dollars.

I say "most of us," as some individuals believe otherwise, which is why we are here. Not specifying the amounts or any other context for the topic was deliberate because no matter the amount, the appropriate response is still false. In a healthy relationship, you shouldn't have to ask your partner about the twenty dollars because you would inherently have an understanding with your partner and a level of financial independence that gives you the discretion to make some financial decisions independently. However, you would discuss with your partner before lending twenty thousand dollars because it would likely exceed an agreed-upon threshold for disclosure. Establishing these boundaries is ultimately the approach you should take, and teaching and reinforcing that approach is the reason why this topic is relevant and important.

Make no mistake: lending money to a relative or anyone without first speaking or having an understanding with your partner is, indeed, a form of financial infidelity. The key word is transparency, and part of having an understanding with your partner about lending money is the purpose of establishing a process that allows for visibility into transactions that could materially impact your finances. Making major financial decisions without consulting your partner undermines the trust in the relationship, regardless of whether the intentions were noble, like helping a relative out of a bind.

I recently watched a television show where a spouse decided to post bail for a relative by putting the house as collateral without telling their significant other. The relative then decided to skip bail. Now I realize this was television, but the outrage I felt watching this episode was real. At that moment, I realized something about human emotions. Oftentimes, our emotions get the best of us. Sometimes, we make decisions purely out of an emotional sense of duty or responsibility for a family member, and perhaps that unique quality is what makes you a good person. It might also be the reason why your family members call on you and/or take advantage of your goodwill. I'm not here to tell you not to bail your family members out of jail, but make sure you involve your partner in making that decision.

WHY THERE'S CONFLICT

Making unilateral financial decisions is a sure way to create conflict in your relationship, especially if those decisions impact the financial well-being of both you and your partner. That type of unilateral decision brings up the issue of family boundaries and how not establishing or crossing those boundaries can ruin your relationship. Not allowing your partner to have a say in the matter can create feelings of betrayal and exclusion, leading to resentment and a breakdown in trust, affecting other areas of the relationship. Just because it is family does not give you the right to make that decision on your own, even if the money is solely yours. That last sentence might be a hard pill to swallow for some of you, but it's why we're here: to address these issues and get you to a state of harmony in your relationship.

DISCUSSION POINTS

1. Emphasize that financial decisions impact both of you and should be approached as a team. Highlight how joint decision-making strengthens your partnership.

2. Create a process for keeping each other informed about significant financial decisions.

3. Talk about your shared financial goals and how lending money might impact them. Consider how such decisions can affect your financial stability and your ability to meet your obligations.

4. Emphasize the importance of respecting each other's perspectives and consulting one another before making decisions that affect both of you.

5. Discuss the need to set boundaries when it comes to lending money to family. Explore what both of you are comfortable with regarding financially supporting relatives.

29

I CAN MAKE LARGE PURCHASES WITHOUT CONSULTING MY PARTNER

Making large purchases without consulting your partner is not ideal. The preferred response is false.

WHY IT MATTERS

When you were single, you made a lot of important financial decisions. You were a responsible adult making informed decisions that benefited you. Now that you're in a long-term relationship, you're being told to shift your approach to making decisions to involve your partner, regardless of whether they are equally as financially savvy as you or not. Failing to consult your partner runs the risk of upending your relationship. This is the common sentiment I see when talking about this particular topic. For some individuals, transitioning from "I" to "Us" is not easy. You might find yourself torn between wanting to make decisions on your own versus taking the time to involve your partner in making joint decisions. You may feel that making decisions on your own is easier. Still, those decisions will ultimately not be in the partnership's best interest.

Admittedly, this was quite challenging for me, and it took a great deal of patience and a willingness to build a true partnership for me to make that transition. Before getting married, I was reluctant to involve my partner in any financial decisions. It was a learning process for me, and she was the one to teach me. You see, even though I was in a long-term relationship, I hadn't fully understood the concept of partnership and that it covered all aspects, not just deciding what restaurant to have dinner or what movie to watch at the theater. I realized this when I decided it was time to pull the trigger on an overdue renovation project. I had some failing balconies that needed to be overhauled as they were no longer safe to go out on. The decision to complete the project wasn't the issue, as I had openly discussed the need to complete the project for quite some time. The real test of our partnership came during the process of selecting the contractor, selecting the materials, and, yes, deciding on what colors to go with. At first, I had it all mapped out. I proudly presented the initial plan to her, and to my shock, she got upset with me. I did not include her in any of the initial planning, which was a problem. She said I wasn't truly committed to the partnership and that it wasn't fair for me to make so many decisions she'd eventually have to live with.

As the viral meme saying goes: "It was at that moment he knew he f*cked up!" She was absolutely right, and I was still operating from an individualistic mindset. Making these decisions without consulting my partner ran the risk of causing major disruption in my relationship. While it seemed to me to be an individual decision, the results had a big implication on our shared life. It's not just about the money; it's about feeling included in decisions that affect both of us. She taught me that consulting her shows respect for her opinions and reinforces the bond built by open communication and transparency. It reinforces the idea that we're a team and that we're working to create a future together.

WHY THERE'S CONFLICT

Imagine your partner coming home with a brand-new car and saying to you, "Surprise!" This unlikely event would seem like a fairytale story, especially if they bought that new car for you. If you go on social media, you are flooded with posts and reels of people surprising their significant other with a new car or some other large purchase as a show of gratitude and how much they care.

These grand gestures are considered "relationship goals" or #relationshipgoals in the social media world. These images, if you believe them to be true, often reinforce the type of money management behavior that we're trying to fix. I use this example because it's no different if you made a large purchase for yourself or your partner. The fact is, you didn't consult each other in the process. Now, I'm not naïve; I believe the images you see on social media are completely staged to attract views. However, there are people out in the real world who believe that striving for that lifestyle is acceptable and desirable. In the real world, you might make a major purchase—like a new car—only to come home and have your partner ask whether you can actually afford it and why you made such a big decision without discussing it first. Listen, I wasn't even able to go out and pick an engagement ring on my own, as my fiancé made it clear that she needed to be part of the process of selecting something she was going to wear for the rest of her life. The bottom line is this: learning how to involve your partner in large purchases can and will help you avoid conflict in your relationship.

DISCUSSION POINTS

1 Discuss the importance of treating financial responsibilities as a joint effort in your relationship.

2 Talk about how a large purchase can affect your overall financial situation and how a unilateral decision can have long-term consequences for both of you.

3 Talk about how consulting each other on big financial decisions strengthens your partnership. Emphasize that it's not about seeking permission but working together as a team.

4 Discuss your shared financial goals and how consulting each other can help achieve them.

5 Discuss the importance of communication and feeling included in decisions that affect both partners. This approach can make you both feel valued and respected in your financial partnership.

30

IT IS OKAY FOR MY PARTNER TO QUESTION HOW I SPEND MONEY

Believe it or not, your partner questioning how you spend money is actually ideal. The preferred response is true.

WHY IT MATTERS

In Topic 23, we discussed the importance of managing financial responsibilities and using a three-step method to accomplish this.

Step 1 – Divide and conquer
Step 2 – Establish a joint account
Step 3 – Check in regularly

In step three, we're talking about the importance of having frequent check-ins at least once per month. During these check-ins, you will have an opportunity to reconcile your budget and check monthly spending. Here is where you will have the chance to have a spirited conversation about your partner's bad spending habits. Well, not exactly. While it is okay to question your partner about their spending habits, there is a right and wrong way to go about doing so. The wrong way could mean you end up on the couch. Before we talk about the right way to go about having this conversation, let's talk a bit more about why it's imperative to review each other's spending.

In any relationship, discussing money can be sensitive, and it might seem that by questioning your partner's spending, you're trying to exhibit some sort of control over them. To be fair, how you approach this could give the impression of wanting control, but more on that later.

Questioning your partner's spending isn't about control; it's about sharing information that provides insights into potential issues such as exceeding your budget or overspending on a particular item or expense. In other words, talking about each other's spending habits is an excellent way of providing a high level of transparency, which is always beneficial for the relationship. It's ultimately about holding each other accountable and keeping an eye on the prize of achieving your shared financial goals. Talking about your spending habits and taking corrective actions will lead to better spending habits and overall financial health. It could also open the door to important conversations about financial stress and how you can better support each other's well-being.

WHY THERE'S CONFLICT

Now, let's go back to the important topic of how to approach your partner about their spending habits. Remember that the wrong way is a fast track to conflict and the living room couch. I will always remember the first time I questioned my wife about her spending habits. Yes, you guessed correctly—this will be a story about how NOT to question your partner about their spending. So, it was a Sunday evening, and I was reconciling the budget. There I was, looking over the credit card statement, and I saw a slew of Amazon purchases. I had noticed Amazon packages showing up quite frequently that month, but I didn't think much of it at the time.

I reviewed the transactions, tallied up the total, and instantly got upset. In my rage, I immediately called my wife on the phone (she was downstairs, by the way), and I immediately went into interrogation mode, asking why there were so many Amazon charges and what on earth she had bought. Needless to say, she didn't respond well to that approach at all, and on top of it all, the purchases were for legitimate items we had discussed months prior, and she was waiting for the items to go on sale during Prime Day. "It was at that moment I knew I f*cked up." It would seem that I'm the villain in every story. Side note: My wife is literally the queen of Amazon and can find a deal like no other. The moral of the story is, don't reconcile your budget on a Sunday evening. In all seriousness, this wasn't the correct approach, and it wasn't the last time I did this. It took several incidents for me to learn how to effectively engage and not confront my wife when questioning her spending. Normalizing a non-confrontational approach can eliminate conflicts when discussing monthly spending habits.

DISCUSSION POINTS

1. If applicable, ask your partner about their views on financial independence and why they may feel that questioning their spending isn't appropriate.
2. Discuss how open communication about spending can help to ensure that both partners are aligned and that you stay on course to achieve your shared financial goals.
3. Discuss how creating transparency builds trust. Questioning spending habits isn't about control; it's about maintaining openness and preventing misunderstandings in the relationship.
4. Discuss how both partners can feel comfortable and respected when having financial discussions moving forward.
5. Discuss how each of you would like to be approached about spending and how you can normalize the conversation.

31

I AM COMFORTABLE DISCLOSING MY INCOME BEFORE MARRIAGE

Disclosing your income before marriage is ideal. The preferred response is true.

WHY IT MATTERS

We've reached the part of the assessment that focuses on your willingness to share key financial information with your partner. I often emphasize the importance of being transparent about your finances before entering a long-term relationship. Most personal finance experts agree that early disclosure is essential, as your financial situation plays a significant role in long-term commitment. Being open from the start can help build a stronger, more balanced partnership. In *Marriage & Finances*, I outline the key aspects of your finances and what you should disclose before marriage.

While all five areas are necessary to disclose, I found that three areas, in particular, were considered more private, and individuals were more inclined to not disclose them and even lie about them. The trifecta of financial information is income, debt, and credit. Typically, your expenses are readily apparent and less likely to be kept a secret, and your assets are usually seen as positive and less likely to be kept hidden. Keep in mind that we already covered how keeping assets like bank accounts a secret is a form of financial infidelity. So, let's first talk about income and why failing to disclose it to your partner can be controversial.

Your income is the revenue you generate to support your lifestyle and financial goals. (3) Most societies place a lot of emphasis on your ability to create value, and our society happens to value money; It's the byproduct of living in a capitalistic society. Our income is often tied to our social status, and it is the gateway to our desired lifestyle. It is safe to say that income plays a vital role in shaping our lives and our relationships. Finding out how much money your partner makes is key to establishing transparency, building trust, and creating a solid foundation for your relationship. Despite what the hopeless romantics may say, money is absolutely an integral part of a partnership.

Income directly influences all other areas of your finances. It determines your ability to pay your living expenses, acquire assets, pay off debt, and improve your credit. It also plays a huge role in defining and shaping your desired future together. This is why sharing your income becomes so important. Knowing how much money each of you makes allows you to set realistic lifestyle expectations. It makes it easier to set realistic goals, especially when combining finances. It will enable you to combine budgets and plan for those big-ticket items, such as saving for a vacation, purchasing a car, or buying your first home. Your income drives your ability to invest and save for your future and retirement.

WHY THERE'S CONFLICT

As I've stated time and time again, money is one of the biggest sources of conflict in relationships, and keeping financial details hidden can lead to unnecessary stress and disagreements. Conversations about income naturally lead to discussions about how each of you views money and the role it plays. These talks often uncover insights into your financial priorities, and sometimes, you may find that your priorities and views about money don't align.

My first conversation with my wife about money happened while we were dating, and needless to say, that conversation did not go very well. We began the conversation by talking about lifestyle expectations and the income required to maintain those expectations. The conversation went well until there was a declaration of expectations for gifts, which wasn't an issue; the issue was the price point of those expected gifts. This is where the argument ensued.

My perspective was that our income didn't reasonably support those expectations, and her rebuttal was that these were reasonable expectations given our income, which at the time was mainly my income. I immediately said that expensive gifts shouldn't be a priority and that it was wrong for her to focus so much on expensive things. It was safe to say we did not see eye to eye, and there was a definite disconnect around income-driven lifestyle expectations. In hindsight, I probably should have read *The Five Love Languages* by Gary Chapman. It would have helped me understand a thing or two. While her primary love language isn't gift-giving (50), it still ranks high on her list.

I was hyper-focused on what an appropriate amount was for a gift. Although my concerns were valid, I realized that she was not expecting me to buy her an expensive handbag every month. It turns out that her primary love language is quality time. (50) This meant that while she had exceptional taste in gifts, her expectations were actually in line with my income, as she was ok receiving the kinds of gifts she wanted once or twice a year instead of every month. I would have never come to this understanding had we not engaged in a conversation early on about income and money expectations. While I may still not fully agree with the exorbitant prices of handbags, working through our differences early on allowed me to understand, appreciate, and accept her standards, and in turn, she did the same for me.

DISCUSSION POINTS

1 Discuss how being aware of each other's financial situation can prevent surprises and potential conflicts. Transparency about income can help avoid misunderstandings and financial stress down the line.

2 Talk about how disclosing income allows you both to set clear expectations regarding lifestyle, savings, and financial responsibilities.

3 Use this as an opportunity to discuss each other's financial values and priorities and how these priorities may change as income increases.

4 Talk about how your income impacts other areas of your finances as it relates to expenses, assets, debt, and credit.

32

I AM COMFORTABLE DISCLOSING MY DEBT BEFORE MARRIAGE

Disclosing your debt before marriage is ideal. The preferred response is true.

WHY IT MATTERS

The second most important aspect of your personal finances that you should disclose is your total debt. Let's face it—most people view debt as a necessary evil in order to attain or maintain a certain lifestyle in today's society. I like to think of debt as a useful and vital tool to create and add value to your life. Debt provides an avenue to acquire assets or take advantage of opportunities that we wouldn't otherwise be able to pay cash for. Acquiring debt does come with risks, as too much of the wrong type of debt can create a spiral of financial ruin.

Most individuals have some form of debt. A study by Experian showed that the average debt carried by single individuals is $51,264. (51) That number alone should be enough to incentivize you to inquire about your partner's debt. But what's even more alarming is the delinquency rate amongst single individuals. That same study found that the portion of delinquent accounts was 32 percent amongst unmarried adults, compared to the national average of 18 percent. (51) Needless to say, being upfront about your debt before getting married is an important step in building a strong and healthy relationship, especially when you're planning to build a future together. "Your ability to use debt wisely sends a positive message to your partner about your ability to manage finances effectively." (3)

We spoke previously in Topic 2 about the importance of having good role models who are cautious about going into debt. We also talked about the importance of thinking twice about taking on excess debt in the name of realizing a dream, such as homeownership. When it comes to debt, what really matters is your everyday approach to debt management, and being honest about debt helps avoid unexpected surprises. Imagine finding out after your wedding that your partner has a substantial student loan or credit card balance; it could create unnecessary tension and make you feel blindsided by something that could have been resolved had they been upfront from the beginning. Your debt also has a direct implication on your credit and your creditworthiness. One way or the other, your debts will come to light, especially if you plan on creating a life with your partner. Openly discussing your debt before marriage shows a willingness to be transparent and a commitment to the success of your partnership and union.

WHY THERE'S CONFLICT

Failing to disclose your debt in a timely manner is a direct line to conflict. Timing is everything, as the amount of debt one carries may very well determine the willingness of someone to commit to something as long-term as marriage. That may seem shallow, but let me be the first to tell you that marriage is not all about love. Marriage is a serious commitment that extends way beyond your feelings for your partner. Now, don't get me wrong, love is absolutely important, but it's quite high maintenance. It turns out that in order to maintain love, you need other things to support it, and your finances are one of those things. Jennifer Lopez once said that her "love don't cost a thing." Well, I think we all know that was a lie, and failing to disclose substantial debt can make you fall out of love quicker than her marriage to Ben Affleck.

A report by Natalie Brown for National Debt Relief agrees with my earlier statements that failing to disclose debt is indeed a form of financial infidelity. She states, "While debt woes can create trouble in any relationship, the problem compounds when one person hides information about debt from the other." (52) Hiding debt has its obvious problems, but entering into a marriage with excess debt also comes with its fair share of problems. However, this should not stop you from disclosing this pertinent information to your partner. As the saying goes, honesty is always the best policy, especially when it comes to disclosing your debts.

DISCUSSION POINTS

1 Talk about how being open about debt builds trust. Transparency with your finances sets a precedent for open communication in other areas.

2 Discuss how knowing about each other's debts allows for effective financial planning. Understanding your combined financial obligations helps you to create a budget and to set achievable goals.

3 Discuss how upfront disclosure prevents future financial surprises. Knowing what to expect financially minimizes potential conflicts and stress later on.

4 Talk about how addressing debt together can strengthen your partnership. Tackling financial challenges as a team shows commitment and reinforces the idea of working together toward common goals.

5 Discuss your financial values and approaches to debt management. Understanding each other's perspectives on debt can help align your financial priorities and goals.

33

I AM COMFORTABLE DISCLOSING MY CREDIT BEFORE MARRIAGE

Disclosing your credit before marriage is ideal.
The preferred response is true.

WHY IT MATTERS

What's your credit score? This question is commonly asked by lenders when seeking a loan. It's the benchmark for credit worthiness and a way of ensuring that you are likely to repay your obligations. Credit is the final piece of the financial trifecta that can lead to conflict if not disclosed before marriage. You need it to finance that car you've been eyeing, to qualify for a mortgage on your dream home—and, if you've been paying attention, it seems you shouldn't tie the knot without discussing it either. Personally, I think getting married without knowing your partner's credit is like buying a used car without looking at the CARFAX™. That analogy might offend some, but it makes sense if you think about it.

Interestingly, the data suggests that a significant number of individuals don't know their partner's credit score prior to marriage. In a survey done by Experian, they found that 40 percent of respondents said they did not know their spouse's credit score before getting married. (53) That's a staggering number, making credit the most undisclosed financial information out of all the other pieces of information. I can't emphasize enough the importance of discussing your credit with your partner before marriage. As mentioned earlier, your credit is a key factor that impacts lifestyle decisions like buying a home or a car. Your credit score is a direct reflection of your financial habits and your ability to manage financial responsibilities. Knowing each other's credit score helps set realistic expectations, allowing you to make smarter choices and to set realistic financial goals that are more achievable. You should provide a copy of your credit report along with a credit score. You can obtain a free copy of your credit report at www.annualcreditreport.com. (3) Most credit cards also provide free access to your credit score and report on a monthly basis.

WHY THERE'S CONFLICT

It's no wonder so many marriages fail. Keeping your credit score a secret runs the risk of creating barriers that impact both you and your partner. Bad credit by itself is a reason for conflict, and finding out after the fact is especially disappointing. Let's face it—we're not perfect, but we can work together to help each other become a better version of ourselves. That is what partnership and marriage is all about. Disclosing your credit early on, whether good or bad, gives you and your partner the opportunity to create a plan that includes improving your credit to ensure that when the time comes, you have access to the best lending options available.

DISCUSSION POINTS

1. Talk about the fact that knowing each other's credit score helps to build trust and transparency in the relationship.

2. Highlight how knowing each other's credit scores can help with effective financial planning. It allows you to make informed decisions about future financial endeavors, like buying a home or car.

3. Discuss how knowing each other's credit scores helps set realistic expectations for your financial future together. It influences the types of loans you can get and the interest rates you'll face.

4 Discuss how sharing this information can help align your values and financial goals. It opens up an important dialogue about how each of you manages credit and debt.

34

MY KNOWLEDGE OF FINANCES IS LIMITED, AND I WOULD PREFER MY PARTNER TO HANDLE THEM

Having a limited knowledge of finances and making your partner handle it is less than ideal. The preferred response is false.

WHY IT MATTERS

As we discussed in Topic 23, relying solely on one person to handle all the finances is not the ideal way to manage your finances in a relationship. While being transparent about your limited knowledge of finances is appropriate, it should not be your reason for not being involved in financial decisions that impact your day-to-day and your long-term well-being. A study by Fidelity Investments showed that many couples still have one partner take the lead for day-to-day finances. (54) The study showed that 24 percent of men said they were the primary decision maker, while 21 percent of women said they were the primary decision maker for day-to-day finances. (54) The study also showed that 57 percent of women indicated that their partner was more knowledgeable of finances, while 31 percent of men indicated that their partner was more knowledgeable of finances. (54)

Relying solely on your partner to handle all the finances because of your limited knowledge might seem convenient, but it also means you may forfeit your seat at the table when it comes to making some of the most important decisions regarding your financial well-being. It's completely normal to feel intimidated by numbers and financial jargon, but taking steps to overcome these fears can significantly benefit your personal development. In *Marriage & Finances*, I emphasize the need for financial literacy in order to ensure a successful partnership. Incorporating financial literacy in your relationship is about having a general understanding of the financial concepts that impact your financial well-being. Understanding concepts such as budgeting and saving and actively making informed decisions about your day-to-day finances leads to increased financial stability and relationship satisfaction.

Sharing financial responsibilities is essential for keeping things equal in a relationship. When both partners pitch in to manage the finances, it ensures that decisions are made fairly and that both your opinions matter. Learning about basic financial concepts enables you to be more proactive with your finances, and it can boost your confidence to participate actively in financial discussions. Learning how to manage your finances also prepares you for life's unexpected events, from an unexpected expense, a job loss, or a health issue, and understanding your financial situation helps you deal with these challenges more confidently and with less stress.

WHY THERE'S CONFLICT

A lack of financial literacy is a primary reason for conflict in any relationship. Conflict can arise for several reasons when it comes to financial literacy. But when we look closer, we can narrow the conflict down to a specific issue. Suppose your partner cannot effectively engage in financial matters. In that case, it may cause you to lose faith in their ability to manage even their own finances. You may see them as a financial liability and someone you have to micromanage in order to ensure your finances stay on track. You may even feel as though you have to treat them like a child when it comes to money matters, operating as a parental figure instead of a partner. In situations where one partner is more financially savvy, conflict often arises from the high expectations they place on the other—expectations rooted in what they see as basic financial knowledge, without recognizing that these assumptions are shaped by their own experience and expertise.

This is equivalent to a colleague at work with years of experience putting expectations on you, a recent grad with little to no experience. You would feel underqualified and intimidated by the role, and you would likely not succeed. But if you were placed in a more junior role, it would allow you to learn and develop while still providing value. This is exactly how you should treat your partner when they have less-than-ideal levels of financial literacy. You would help them learn while allowing them to add value by participating in the financial management process. Allow them to take ownership of smaller tasks until they become comfortable taking on larger ones. This teamwork helps prevent any power struggles and builds mutual respect. Plus, it prevents any resentment that might come up if one person is left handling all the finances.

DISCUSSION POINTS

1. If applicable, encourage your partner to learn more about finances. Share how gaining knowledge about budgeting, saving, and investing can be empowering and boost their confidence.

2. Talk about the importance of financial literacy and how it can help avoid dependency on the more financially savvy individual.

3. Highlight that you're in this together and that you can support each other as a team by providing opportunities for each other to participate in the financial management process.

4. Offer to learn together, perhaps by reading Marriage & Finances: The Three-Day Guide to Financial Literacy to Prepare for a Successful Union.

35

I WOULD ALWAYS BE HONEST WITH MY PARTNER ABOUT HOW I SPEND MONEY

Being honest with your partner about how you spend money is always ideal. The preferred response is <u>true</u>.

WHY IT MATTERS

In Topic 30, we talked about normalizing the act of discussing your spending habits and how to go about asking your partner about their spending. Now we're tackling a common issue in relationships, and that is the tendency for individuals to lie about their spending habits. Spending is and always will be a point of contention in most relationships. We may not always agree on where our partners spend their money. I have come to accept the fact that my wife has a love affair with the Amazon delivery driver, as there seems to be a package at the door daily. The reality is that, provided we're living within our budget and meeting our financial goals, what she spends her discretionary funds on is entirely up to her. But in that same regard, if I were to inquire into those purchases, it is reasonable to expect that she would be honest with me about what she's buying.

Remember, lying about spending habits is considered a form of financial infidelity. In Topic 25, we discussed a recent survey by Bankrate that identified overspending as the most common aspect of finances that individuals lie about. The survey found that 33 percent of individuals in a committed relationship have spent more than their partner would be comfortable with. (44) This is a pervasive issue, and lying about spending habits can exacerbate problems, especially if you're already having a difficult time managing your budget. Being honest with your partner about how you spend money is about establishing a foundation of complete transparency and mutual respect for each other, reinforcing that theme of partnership. Being upfront about your spending shows your partner that you value them. It's a way of saying, "I respect you enough to share everything, even the uncomfortable stuff."

WHY THERE'S CONFLICT

A relationship is built on honesty. It's about trusting each other as you work toward your shared goals. If one person is hiding their spending, it can throw the whole plan off and jeopardize achieving those goals. The tricky thing about hiding your spending is it tends to start small then snowballs into a much larger problem. One day, it's buying a few odds and ends, and before you know it, you've got a whole storage locker full of expansive bottles of whiskey that you don't want your wife to know you have.

This may seem farfetched, but this was actually the dilemma a friend of mine faced as he had both an expensive and potentially unhealthy habit of collecting whiskey. From rare American bourbons to pricey Highland Scotch, you name it, he probably had at least two bottles of it. Eventually, his "hobby" came to light, and the discovery almost led to divorce. Fortunately for him, his wife was really understanding and was more concerned about why he felt he had to hide and not share all the good stuff with her than she was about the financial infidelity.

Honesty is truly the best policy. Ted Rossman, a senior industry analyst at Bankrate, said it best: "Money secrets can undermine a relationship. It's hard enough to meet your financial goals when you're pulling in the same direction. It's almost impossible if you're pulling in opposite directions." (44) Financial infidelity doesn't have to ruin your relationship if you establish the right expectations upfront. When you combine this with a system of transparency, you can work together to prevent the need to feel like you have to hide your spending from your partner. Having a mutual interest in the success of your finances is fundamentally intertwined with the success of your relationship.

In my attempt to make a spin on the lyrics to the song *Love and Marriage* by Frank Sinatra, (55) I'll leave you with this little nugget:

> *"Marriage and finance, marriage and finance,*
> *They go together like a horse and carriage.*
> *This I tell you, brother (and sister),*
> *You can't have one without the other."*

DISCUSSION POINTS

1 Discuss how transparency can help to prevent conflicts. When both partners are aware of each other's spending, it reduces the likelihood of surprises.

2 Discuss how sharing spending habits can lead to better financial management and decision-making as a couple.

3 Highlight how being honest about your spending habits helps align your financial goals and priorities.

4 Talk about how secrecy around spending can lead to feelings of resentment or betrayal if discovered.

5 Point out that financial dishonesty can add unnecessary stress to the relationship.

6 Talk about the benefits of creating a budget together, which requires honesty about spending. A joint budget allows both partners to feel involved and accountable for financial decisions.

7 Discuss establishing a monthly cadence for sitting down and reviewing your credit card or bank statements.

36

I SET ASIDE A PORTION OF EACH PAYCHECK TO GO TOWARD SAVINGS

Setting aside a portion of each paycheck to go toward savings is ideal. The preferred response is true.

WHY IT MATTERS

Having some level of savings is like having a safety net. Life loves to throw curveballs. From car repairs or surprise medical bills, having a stash of cash ready means you won't be scrambling or stressing out trying to figure out how you're going to pay for it. It's definitely a huge relief knowing you've got something to fall back on. However, the problem is that folks are finding it difficult to allocate money to go toward savings, and they don't necessarily place emphasis on putting money aside from each paycheck. According to a survey conducted by Bankrate, 34 percent of Millennials say they live life paycheck to paycheck, compared to 40 percent of Gen X and 28 percent of Gen Z. (56)

Establishing a savings plan is the first step toward achieving your savings goals. There are four steps to creating a savings plan. The steps include determining your savings objective, establishing a savings target, choosing a savings account, and monitoring your savings plan. (3)

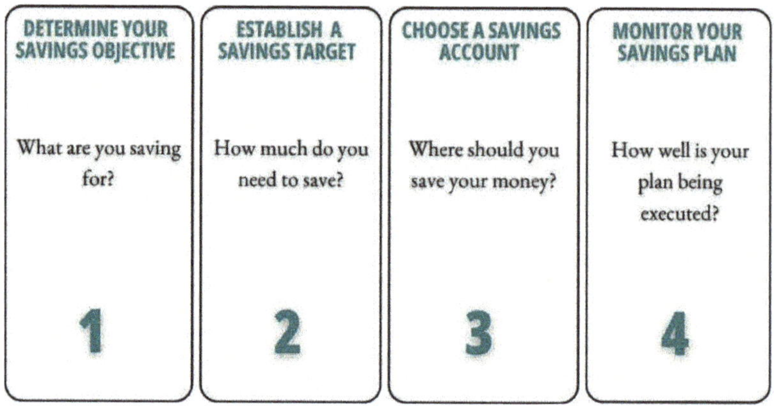

Now that your plan is in place, let's discuss some methods that you can use to help you save money at each paycheck. One method is to pay yourself first. This means setting aside a specific amount for savings as soon as your paycheck hits your account. Treat this savings allocation like any other bill. You can even automate the process by setting up a direct deposit with your payroll administrator or setting up an automated transfer from your checking account to a high-yield savings account. Another method is to consider using percentages to save instead of a fixed dollar amount.

A good rule of thumb is to save between 10 and 20 percent of each paycheck, but feel free to adjust it based on your financial goals. Using a percentage in lieu of a fixed dollar amount will allow your savings to increase as your income rises. A third method to consider is the savings-by-category method. This method uses specific categories to break down your savings into specific purposes, like an emergency fund, a vacation, or a retirement account. This makes the act of saving feel more purpose-driven versus an arbitrary amount or percentage. You can allocate different percentages or amounts from each paycheck to each category based on your priorities. This method not only keeps you organized but also keeps you motivated as you get closer to realizing each goal.

Personally, I use a fixed amount that comes directly from my paycheck and goes directly into a high-yield savings account (HYSA). That amount currently works out to be between 15 and 20 percent of my salary that I put toward savings—17 percent to be exact. No matter the method you choose, you should always consider lifestyle adjustments that can free up cash to maximize savings. Review your budget to identify areas where you can cut back. Perhaps it's dining out less often or canceling subscriptions you don't use regularly. Reallocating this money toward savings can make a big difference over time without making unreasonable compromises to your quality of life, giving you that extra help toward achieving your savings goals.

WHY THERE'S CONFLICT

There's a saying that goes, "More money, more problems." Well, I'm going to respectfully disagree. Instead the saying should be, "No money, more problems." Conflict is inevitable when you have no savings. It doesn't matter what the reason is for not saving; you are bound to run into financial issues at some point—issues that you could have solved had you had some level of savings. I know this might seem idealistic to some, so let's get real for a moment. I realize that many of you may have various circumstances that inhibit you from allocating money toward savings on a regular basis. Financial hardship is real, and I am not naïve enough to think you can save your way out of everything like a lot of personal finance experts might want to have you think.

While we all can acknowledge the importance of saving, life happens. You could be in a situation where you were laid off and had to take a lower-paying job to make ends meet. Or you could be faced with a situation where you have had to deplete your savings to pay for medical expenses for yourself or a loved one. This book is intended to be a preventative measure, giving you tips and solutions to help mitigate potential problems down the road. If you or your partner is experiencing extreme financial hardship, then there is help for you. That help may not necessarily be within the covers of this book. My next book might very well be about proven strategies to get out of various financial hardships. No matter the circumstance, your goal should always be to work toward a solution that allows you to once again live below your means.

DISCUSSION POINTS

1. Discuss each other's current method for managing your savings and highlight the benefits of your chosen method.

2. Discuss the benefits of developing a good savings plan and how it has or can positively impact your financial well-being.

3. If you haven't yet implemented a savings plan, talk about ways to incorporate savings into your budget. Discuss how much to allocate for savings and automate with direct deposit.

37

I MAKE CONTRIBUTIONS TO A RETIREMENT ACCOUNT

Making regular contributions to a retirement account such as a 401K or IRA, is more than ideal. The preferred response is true.

WHY IT MATTERS

Let's talk about why contributing to a retirement account is one of the best financial moves you can make for your future. It might not be the most exciting topic, but your future self will thank you. First off, think of a retirement account as a time machine for your money. The earlier you start, the more time your money has to grow. Thanks to the beauty of compound interest, even small contributions can grow into a sizable nest egg. It's like planting a tree; the sooner you plant it, the more time it has to grow into something substantial. One of the most compelling reasons to have a retirement account is the ability to access the tax advantages that come with it. You can lower your tax burden at the time of contribution if you select certain types of accounts, or you can take tax-free distributions on other types of accounts upon retirement age. It is quite nice to receive a small gift from Uncle Sam for being a diligent person in managing one's finances. Who doesn't love a good tax break? Also, who can't use some peace of mind? Life is unpredictable, and having a proper retirement plan is something that gives you the assurance that all is well and you will be fine, even in the future. It is comforting to know that you are planning for a comfortable life during your retirement without having to stress over how you will meet your financial needs.

Contributing to a retirement account is about preserving your freedom. It is about being able to do the things you want to do in life. It's about being able to travel, do what you love, and spend quality time with loved ones. This is why it is important to save money now so that in the future, you will be able to make decisions about how you want to live your life without being limited by financial burdens.

"If you fail to plan, you are planning to fail."

– Benjamin Franklin

WHY THERE'S CONFLICT

Nothing says conflict more than not having enough money to retire on, and couples often make mistakes when it comes to retirement. Below, you'll find a list of some common mistakes to avoid when planning for retirement. (3)

Starting late	The earlier you start saving and investing for retirement, the more time your money has to grow through compound interest. Starting late may require higher savings rates or result in a smaller retirement nest egg.
Relying solely on Social Security	Relying only on Social Security benefits for retirement income may be risky. Social Security is meant to supplement retirement savings and not to provide complete financial security. It's important to have other sources of income like personal savings, pensions, or investments.
Insufficient 401K contributions	Make sure to contribute enough to your employer's matching program to receive the full match. This is essentially free money and can greatly increase your savings.

Ignoring inflation	Inflation causes the value of money to decrease over time, resulting in higher expenses in the future. To accurately estimate your retirement savings needs, it's crucial to take inflation into account.
Not diversifying investments	Diversification helps reduce the potential impact of market volatility and spreads out risk. It's important to have a well-diversified portfolio that includes different types of assets.
Not accounting for age gaps	While retiring together seems most appealing, there are circumstances that may require one partner to continue working to maximize their retirement benefits. It's important to factor in the time to retire for both partners when establishing your plan.
Failing to adjust the plan	Failure to review and adjust the retirement plan regularly can lead to faulty assumptions and inadequate savings. It's important to reassess and make necessary adjustments to the plan as needed.
Underestimating healthcare costs	Failing to account for rising healthcare costs can result in financial strain. Make sure to account for added healthcare costs and consider options such as long-term care insurance.
Not having an emergency fund	You may have to tap into your retirement savings if you do not have an emergency fund, and this can potentially lead to financial difficulties. It's wise to have a separate emergency fund to cover any unexpected expenses.

DISCUSSION POINTS

1 Discuss how starting to save now can help ensure a comfortable lifestyle in the future, allowing both of you to enjoy your retirement years without financial worries.

2 Talk about how you envision your retirement. You can create a retirement vision board to help visualize your retirement. Use the SMART goals method to establish your retirement goals.

3 Discuss ways you can plan to avoid some of the common mistakes made when planning for retirement.

4 Explore the tax benefits of various retirement accounts. Depending on the type of account, contributions might lower taxable income now, or withdrawals might be tax-free later.

5 Review your budget to identify areas where you can cut back and redirect funds toward retirement savings.

6 Consider meeting with a financial advisor to discuss retirement options and create a personalized retirement savings plan.

PART THREE

HOW YOU PLAN TO TEACH YOUR CHILDREN ABOUT MONEY AND FINANCES

38

CHILDREN SHOULD LEARN THE VALUE OF MONEY

Teaching your kids about the value of money is more than ideal. The preferred response is true.

WHY IT MATTERS

Teaching your kids about the value of money is one of the most important lessons they can learn from you. It's not just about dollars and cents; it's about setting them up to be financially independent and preparing them for a lifetime of financial decisions that will impact their lives and the lives of others.

Nowadays, it has become increasingly important for individuals to be financially conscious as our financial systems have become more and more complex. This is why teaching kids about finance at a young age is so crucial. The sooner they learn, the more equipped they become to take on what the world throws at them. Even teaching them how to budget their allowance to save up for a new toy is a skill set that will help them in the future when it comes to bigger and more critical decisions. When children understand the value of money through the process of earning, saving, and spending the money they have, they become accountable for their actions. It teaches them the value of money and the effort required to earn it. They realize that money does not simply "grow on trees," and they develop a mindset of being more cautious with their choices.

WHY THERE'S CONFLICT

As parents, you need to approach the process of teaching your children how to manage money on a united front, much like everything else parents teach their kids. Teaching and leading by example are crucial. If one or both parents have poor spending habits, then it's likely that your child will pick up those habits as well. There is no bigger shock than when you accept delivery of twenty pizzas because your child got a hold of your phone and went crazy on Uber Eats. This is the point where you have to decide to take the calmer route and make it a teachable moment for your child and yourself.

The burden of your child's transgressions falls on you, the parent. Oftentimes, as parents, we may find ourselves arguing over situations that our children may find themselves in. Not having a united approach to teaching your kids about money can pit partners against each other. For example, one partner may allow the child to spend money more freely while the other partner would rather they save their money. One partner might want them to earn their money, while another is fine with giving them an allowance. It's that cliché scenario where the child asks one parent for something, and when that parent says no, they go to the other parent to get a yes.

No matter what your parenting style differences are, it's vital that you compromise on an approach that is representative of each of your values and consistent in reinforcing good money habits to your children at an early age.

DISCUSSION POINTS

1. Discuss how learning about money can teach children responsibility and independence.
2. Highlight how understanding the value of money can instill a strong work ethic and help develop critical decision-making skills.
3. Talk about the importance of preparing children for future financial responsibilities, such as paying bills, managing credit, and saving for big expenses.

4 Discuss how teaching children the value of money can help them avoid common financial pitfalls, such as excessive debt or impulsive spending.

39

I PLAN TO SHARE MY FINANCIAL SITUATION WITH MY CHILDREN

Sharing your financial situation with your children is ideal. The preferred response is true.

WHY IT MATTERS

Sharing your finances with your children may seem unconventional, but there is some real value in being this transparent. From household finances to taxes, showing your kids what's behind the curtain is a way to demystify money for your kids. Ron Lieber said it best in his book, *The Opposite of Spoiled: Raising Kids Who Are Grounded, Generous, and Smart About Money.* The reason why many parents do not share finances with their kids is due to a strong belief that talking about money isn't age appropriate. (57) He encourages adults to get rid of that old-fashioned way of thinking and to be open to children asking questions about money. He also acknowledges that there is an inherent fear that adults may have of not having enough knowledge to answer the questions kids may have, which may deter parents from engaging in such conversations. That is why it's so important to have a level of financial literacy, as it not only benefits you and your ability to navigate your finances, but it also helps you educate others, namely your children.

As uncomfortable as it may feel to talk money with our kids, it's worth it when we view it as part of nurturing critical skills for future self-sufficiency. (58) Involving your child in certain aspects of managing the household finances teaches them about the reality of money while they are young, allowing them to have a better view of how financial systems work in the real world. It is also important to discuss financial issues that can help establish appropriate expectations. It helps your children understand the financial values that are held in the family with regard to spending and saving money. These lessons are important as they will help in the development of financial stability and independence.

WHY THERE'S CONFLICT

As parents, you will need to come to an agreement on the level of transparency you plan to have with your children about your finances. Your own childhood and your parents' approach to exposing you to finances play a big role in determining your willingness and ability to be transparent with your kids. My wife and I plan on being very deliberate about how we share our finances, with the goal of teaching our only child about finances from a young age. We've agreed on what information we will share and when. This wasn't easy, particularly for my wife, as she felt that too much exposure to "adult issues" placed an undue amount of stress on her for things she didn't understand as a child.

Needless to say, we were not on the same page at first. I wanted to be fully transparent with money as a way to immerse them in life's greatest lessons. Or so I thought. The reality is that the more effective way is to approach our child's exposure to finances in small steps, get down on their level, and introduce small aspects of finances by involving them in activities that will inspire them and pique their interest in the matter, putting them in the driver's seat in learning about money and having fun at the same time.

DISCUSSION POINTS

1 Discuss how transparency can remove the mystery of financial matters for your children. By understanding the family's financial dynamics, they are less likely to develop misconceptions or anxiety about money.

2 Explain how involving children in financial discussions can teach them responsibility. They learn to appreciate the costs of living and the effort required to manage money wisely, which can lead to better financial habits.

3 Discuss how sharing financial details allows you to model positive financial behaviors. Your children can learn from your experiences and see firsthand how to handle finances effectively and responsibly.

40

CHILDREN SHOULD BE GIVEN THE CHANCE TO MANAGE THEIR OWN MONEY

Giving children the chance to manage their own money is ideal. The preferred response is true.

WHY IT MATTERS

It may seem a bit intimidating to let children handle their own finances. Still, it is an important aspect of their financial education. The responsibility of managing money is a great way to learn. It's one thing to explain and lecture them about money management, but it becomes more real when they handle their own finances. Whether it is an allowance or cash earned from doing chores, having money in their own right allows them to learn the ins and outs of money. A study published in *Family Relations* found the importance of hands-on learning and the added benefits for children regarding finances. According to the study, the best thing parents can do is to give their kids opportunities for experiential learning, which will let them manage their own finances and practice making financial decisions. Kids who learn from their mistakes are more likely to be comfortable making financial decisions as young adults. (59)

When kids are allowed to manage their money, they are able to understand the value of money. They get to learn the process of earning it and the need to spend it wisely. They get to learn hands-on how to consider the options of what is and isn't important and feel the consequences of their decisions. These lessons are vital and are not just limited to money and finances but other aspects of life as well. Managing their own money also helps them develop a sense of independence and confidence. Kids feel empowered when they are allowed to make decisions independently, especially decisions that affect the ability to purchase something they want. As adults, we know how difficult these decisions can be, and even the savviest of us make mistakes. Allowing our kids to have some independence to handle their own money allows them to make mistakes and learn from them. This is why it is so important that, as parents, we help our children understand that sometimes they will make wrong decisions. We must guide them through the learning process so that they can become the next generation of financially savvy adults.

WHY THERE'S CONFLICT

The benefits are clear: Hands-on learning is more effective than lecturing kids about money and finances. Interestingly enough, a difference in approach is the very thing that causes conflicts among parents. One parent will want to sit and talk through the process of setting up a savings account, while the other parent prefers to go to the bank in person and show them the process. There are certainly merits to both approaches. While the hands-on approach is preferred, we can't dismiss the benefits of talking through the process before physically setting up the savings account. Remember, I'm not advocating that the hands-on approach is best for all learning. It should go without saying that certain lessons can't be hands-on. I am only talking about the benefits of hands-on learning as it pertains to money and finances.

As a child, I recall a clear distinction between my mother's and father's approaches. My mother was a school teacher, and my father was an engineer, so it couldn't be more obvious who was the lecturer and who was hands-on. I also recall them having quite a few disagreements as a result of their very different approaches to parenting. My wife often tells me that I'm a true hybrid of my parents as I am both a lecturer and hands-on. What's important is that she appreciates those qualities, and we understand the importance of agreeing on the best approach for teaching our kids about life's most important lessons.

DISCUSSION POINTS

1. Discuss ways in which you plan to give your children opportunities to manage their own money. At what age would you start allowing them to manage their own money?

2. Discuss how managing their own money provides children with real-world financial experience and how giving kids control over their own money helps them understand its value.

3. Talk about how managing money helps kids develop critical decision-making skills about how to spend their money and the consequences of poor decisions.

4. Talk about how having their own money fosters independence and confidence and gives children the chance to make mistakes in a safe environment.

41

MY CHILDREN SHOULD PAY FOR THEIR OWN COLLEGE EDUCATION

Making your children pay for their own college education is less than ideal. The preferred response is false.

WHY IT MATTERS

For our final topic, we saved the best for last. Paying for your child's college education should be a priority if you can afford it. The relief of this significant financial burden is a benefit that gives your children a financial leg up upon graduation instead of facing years, if not decades, of paying off student loans, limiting their ability to start their adult lives on solid financial ground. Furthermore, covering your children's college expenses isn't just about relieving them of this significant financial burden; it allows them to focus on their studies. In many ways, college is the formative period of one's life, both educationally and personally, and having to work long hours to meet tuition expenses can be very distracting. By supporting them financially, you enable them to focus on their studies, enrichment activities, and friendships that they may form in college, which can be helpful in the future.

The reality is not all parents can pay, or plan to pay, for their kid's tuition, leaving their kids to foot most or all of the bill. In 2019, a survey from Discover Student Loans showed that only 28 percent of parents said they would cover the entire cost of their child's college education. (60) This survey was conducted amongst parents with children who were nearing college. The startling data shows the magnitude of the number of young people headed to college with the burden of footing the bill themselves, often in the form of student loans. The survey also indicated that these parents were unwilling or unable to pay using money from savings or from a college savings plan. (60) Although the survey did not draw any conclusions as to the reason, one can conclude that the underlying reason for the inability to pay stems from inadequate savings from both personal savings and a college savings plan.

The cost of higher education continues to increase from year to year. Many young adults who want to go to college are left with no choice but to take on thousands in student loan debt. According to the *U.S. News & World Report* data for 2024–2025, the average cost of tuition and fees to attend a ranked public college in-state is $11,011, compared with $43,505 for a ranked private college and $24, 513 for out-of-state students at public colleges. (61) This is even more reason for your family planning goals to include a plan to cover some, if not all, of your child's higher education, should they choose to go. (3)

The earlier you can start saving for your child's education, the better. Even small contributions can add up over time. Consider the following steps when planning to save for your child's higher education. *Marriage & Finances* provides a quick reference to help get you started.

ESTABLISH YOUR EDUCATION SAVINGS GOAL

Determine how much you need to save for your child's education.

1

DETERMINE YOUR SAVINGS AND INVESTMENT VEHICLE

Consider opening a tax-advantaged savings plan.

2

CONTRIBUTE MONTHLY TOWARD YOUR GOAL

Prioritize putting aside a monthly amount toward your goal.

3

Saving for your child's education is easier than you think. With a 529 account, you can save as little or as much as you want, but ideally, you want to have a target in mind and start early. A 529 plan is a tax-advantaged account for education savings. It covers college, K-12, and student loans. The earnings and withdrawals are tax-free if used for qualified education expenses. Most states offer 529 plans, and you can usually choose a plan from another state. Choosing a plan has never been easier. You can go to helpful sites like *Savingforcollege.com* and learn everything you need to learn about 529 plans. Look at the investment options and fees to make an informed decision and select the right plan for you.

WHY THERE'S CONFLICT

The other drawback of not being able to pay for your child's education is the increased instability that will occur with your own finances. Whether you can afford it or not, a financial obligation will exist if your child decides to go to college. If we've learned one thing, it is that with additional financial obligations comes stress and inevitable conflict, which is why planning for the future and starting early is so important. Creating an environment where your child can focus on their education—without the stress of wondering whether tuition will be paid before the registration deadline—supports both your peace of mind and the health of your relationship. Now, I know that many of you may say this may not be practical for all, and the math doesn't add up for everyone. Well, let's do some math, shall we?

Investing $300 monthly for 18 years in an S&P 500-indexed investment portfolio would yield over $180,000 if your average annual return matches the current 18-year average of 10.5 percent.

You can achieve a comparable result by investing in a 529 plan and selecting a mutual fund portfolio that invests in broader U.S. equity or stocks. I can personally vouch for the benefits of a 529 plan, as the annual return on my son's 529 plan over the past two years since I opened it has been an average of around 13 percent. The bottom line is if you plan to start a family or already have children, now is the time to prepare for their future and the future of your relationship. Invest now in a stress-free college experience for your child and a conflict-free relationship for yourselves.

DISCUSSION POINTS

1 Talk about the benefits of allowing your child to focus on their education and personal development without the burden of full financial responsibility.

2 Discuss the implications of student debt on their future. Discuss how starting adult life with significant debt might impact their career choices, ability to buy a home, or even start a family, and whether this aligns with your values and hopes for their future.

3 Discuss how you would prioritize saving for your child's education using a 529 plan.

4 Discuss potential compromises, such as your child contributing a portion of their expenses or working part-time to cover certain costs while still receiving your financial support.

5 Discuss how savings, scholarships, or other financial aid options might play a role in this decision.

CREATE YOUR FINANCIAL COMPATIBILITY ACTION PLAN

You have come to the point in the book where you have the opportunity to take all that you've learned and put it together in an action plan that is focused on maintaining financial compatibility in your relationship. The financial compatibility action plan (FCAP) moves you from conflict to harmony. Your FCAP will organize the topics likely to cause conflict and identify objectives and action items to move you and your partner toward the ideal conflict-free approach to each topic. Let's discuss the key components of your FCAP and what to consider when developing your plan.

NARROW DOWN TOPICS THAT ARE CAUSING CONFLICT

Identify the topics you believe are most likely to cause conflict. Use your compatibility matrix and topic review to narrow down the areas you think need attention—either now or in the future—to help avoid conflict. You may rank or prioritize them as you see fit. As you make your selections, consider how each topic aligns with your financial goals. I suggest you prioritize the topics that could potentially prevent you from achieving your shared financial goals. It is likely that you won't need to include topics that cover your childhood experiences. However, it is my hope that through your review of your childhood experiences, you gained a better understanding and appreciation for your partner's experiences and how it has affected their relationship with money. The most important thing to consider is that your selection of topics should be focused on the goal of creating a more harmonious relationship.

ESTABLISH OBJECTIVES TO RESOLVE CONFLICT

Once you have your list of topics, think about the objectives you will need to establish in order to reconcile your differences and achieve alignment with the ideal approach to each topic. Establish action items for each objective that will enable you to achieve the objectives. Your action items should be specific, measurable, achievable, and realistic. You should also establish a timeframe to meet that objective. To illustrate, if your topic is saving for emergencies, your objective would be to establish an emergency fund of 6 months' worth of salary equal to $35,000. The action items would be to open a high yield savings account and setup bi-weekly direct deposits of 20 percent of each paycheck until you reach your goal in approximately 24 months. As I mentioned, your objectives should be focused on accomplishing the ideal approach to each topic. The discussion points for each topic were curated with the intent of helping you and your partner speak through your differences and come to an understanding of the ideal approach. Your discussions should help you develop your objectives for each topic.

The chart below is a sample illustration of a financial compatibility action plan. You can organize your topics and objectives on the provided FCAP template on the following pages.

FINANCIAL COMPATIBILITY ACTION PLAN			
TOPIC	OBJECTIVE	ACTION ITEM	TIMEFRAME
Topic 24: I believe it is important to save.	Establish an emergency fund with a target of 6 months' salary equal to $35,000.	• Open a HYSA account, and setup bi-weekly direct deposit of 20 percent of your salary. • Deposit any additional costs savings into the emergency fund.	Complete emergency fund goal within 18 to 24 months.

1. You can have multiple objectives for each topic.
2. Your action items should correspond to the completion of each objective.
3. The timeframe should correspond to the completion of each objective.

FINANCIAL COMPATIBILITY ACTION PLAN			
TOPIC	OBJECTIVE	ACTION ITEM	TIMEFRAME

FINANCIAL COMPATIBILITY ACTION PLAN			
TOPIC	OBJECTIVE	ACTION ITEM	TIMEFRAME

CONCLUSION

We've come to the end of our journey, and hopefully, you're in a better place now than when you started this book. If you take away anything from this book, it is my hope that it will be the following three things:

1. ***Financial compatibility is about having a joint approach to money and finances.***
2. ***Financial compatibility can and should be measured.***
3. ***Financial compatibility is not static and can be improved.***

You should have a new level of confidence that comes with understanding what it takes to manage conflict and be financially compatible with your partner. So, let's recap what you've learned.

FINANCIAL COMPATIBILITY IS A JOINT APPROACH TO MONEY AND FINANCES

The key term here is "a joint approach." As a couple, you may not agree on everything, but you should always endeavor to compromise and do things that benefit the well-being of the relationship. Compromise is an important concept when it comes to relationships, and when it comes to money and finances, compromise is vital. But when we hear the word compromise in relationships, we often think about it in terms of what each partner has to give up or sacrifice for the sake of the relationship. We learned that financial compatibility is less about compromise and more about understanding and adopting a shared approach that makes it less like sacrifice and more like a collective win.

The ability to take a joint approach to money and finances effectively is the desired result of a financially compatible partnership. Achieving that level of compatibility is what the kids call relationship goals (#relationshipgoals). You first have to understand each other's perspective when it comes to money and finances. This perspective is a culmination of three themes: your experiences growing up, your approach as an adult, and your sentiments on how you plan to teach your children. Ultimately, becoming financially compatible with your partner is a process that involves understanding your current level of compatibility, understanding what might cause conflict in your relationship, and developing a plan to manage conflict and improve compatibility.

FINANCIAL COMPATIBILITY CAN AND SHOULD BE MEASURED

Understanding how genuinely compatible you are with your partner has always been a point of interest for every couple. Knowing your partner's likes and dislikes and if they match yours is just an example of what we do to ensure they are the one. Our interest in compatibility should be no different when it comes to money and finances. You can determine your current level of financial compatibility by utilizing the financial compatibility assessment (FCA). The FCA can clearly identify the topics that you and your partner share a common perspective on and the topics that are likely to cause conflict. Your financial compatibility matrix presents a visual representation of your financial compatibility and clearly depicts the topics that you currently agree on and, more importantly, the topics that can cause conflict.

Having a clear view of your financial compatibility through the lens of the FCA provides a variety of benefits that, if acted upon, will u that much closer to #relationshipgoals. Benefits include:

1. ***Identification of potential conflicts***
2. ***Improved communication***
3. ***Alignment of financial goals***
4. ***Increased understanding***
5. ***Improved financial planning***
6. ***Strengthened relationship***

FINANCIAL COMPATIBILITY IS NOT STATIC AND CAN BE IMPROVED

You can improve your level of financial compatibility by gaining an understanding of the significance of each key topic and how conflict can impact your relationship. Improving financial compatibility is less about what you have in common and more about how you manage conflict. Your ability to manage conflict effectively can make or break your relationship. This is why developing a financial compatibility action plan is vital to helping you improve your compatibility. Creating and implementing an effective plan requires you to review the key topics that influence compatibility thoroughly. It requires you to understand why the topics matter and why there might be conflict and to discuss ways to manage conflict and improve compatibility. The financial compatibility action plan brings it all together; it's your blueprint to financial compatibility that moves your relationship from conflict to harmony.

BIBLIOGRAPHY

1. **Allied Market Research.** Comic Book Market Size, share, Competitive Landscape and Trend Analysis Report, by type, by end user, by distribution channel : Global Opportunity Analysis and Industry Forecast, 2023-2032. *Allied Market Research.* [Online] https://tinyurl.com/358hyssp.

2. *The relationship between conflict topics and romantic relationship dynamics.* **Meyer, Dixie and Sledge, Renata.** 2, March 1, 2021, Journal of Family Issues, Vol. 43, pp. 306-323. https://doi.org/10.1177/0192513x21993856. 10.1177/0192513x21993856.

3. **Waugh, Chae.** *Marriage & Finances: The Three-Day Guide to Financial Literacy to Prepare for a Successful Union.* s.l. : The Spicy Life Inc., 2023.

4. *Reasons for Divorce and Recollections of Premarital Intervention: Implications for Improving Relationship Education.* **Shelby, Scott B., et al.** 2, 2013, Couple and Family Psychology Research and Practice, Vol. 2, pp. 131 - 145. https://europepmc.org/articles/pmc4012696?pdf=render. 10.1037/a0032025.

5. **DiDonato, Theresa E.** Money decisions can affect the health of your relationship. *Psychology Today.* [Online] August 26, 2022. https://www.psychologytoday.com/us/blog/meet-catch-and-keep/202208/are-you-and-your-partner-financially-compatible.

6. **FDIC Resource Center.** Teaching children about money now, pays dividends later. *FDIC.gov.* [Online] https://tinyurl.com/34jfp8yb.

7. *Parental debt and children's socioemotional well-being.* **Berger, Lawrence M. and Houle, Jason N.** 2, January 22, 2016, American Academy of Pediatrics, Vol. 137. https://pediatrics.aappublications.org/content/pediatrics/137/2/e20153059.full.pdf. 10.1542/peds.2015-3059.

8. **Allen, Dr. Sarah S.** Why are some children affected by parental conflict while others are not? *Dr. Sarah Allen Counseling.* [Online] May 18, 2024. https://tinyurl.com/3ntk85nr.

9. **Kearney, Melissa S.** The U.S. economy needs more two parent families. *TIME.* [Online] September 28, 2023. https://time.com/6317692/u-s-economy-two-parent-families/.

10. *The consequences of income instability for Children's Well-Being.* **Hill, Heather D., et al.** 2, January 17, 2023, Child Development Perspectives, Vol. 7, pp. 85-90. https://pmc.ncbi.nlm.nih.gov/articles/PMC7546433/. 10.1111/cdep.12018.

11. **Abrams, Zara (Z.).** Are your kids stressed about family finances? Psychologists offer answers for addressing anxiety over tight budgets. *American Psychological Association.* [Online] April 27, 2023. https://www.apa.org/topics/money/family-financial-strain.

12. *Sense of control under uncertainty depends on people's childhood environment: a Life History Theory approach.* **Mittal, Chiraag C. and Griskevicius, Vladas V.** 4, August 18, 2014, Journal of Personality and Social Psychology, Vol. 107, pp. 621-637. https://doi.org/10.1037/a0037398. 10.1037/a0037398.

13. **Sheehy-Skeffington, Jennifer and Rea, Jessica.** *How poverty affects people's decision-making processes.* Department of Psychological and Behavioural Science (PBS), The London School of Economics and Political Science. s.l. : Joseph Rowntree Foundation, 2017. https://www.lse.ac.uk/PBS/assets/documents/2017-sheehy-and-rea-report-3234-final-1.pdf.

14. *Early life conditions and financial risk-taking in older age.* **Christelis, Dimitris, Dobrescu, Loretti I and Motta, Alberto.** July 18, 2020, The Journal of the Economics of Ageing, Vol. 17, p. 100266. https://doi.org/10.1016/j.jeoa.2020.100266. 10.1016/j.jeoa.2020.100266.

15. **Fay, Bill.** Debt in America: Statistics and demographics. *Debt.org.* [Online] December 4, 2023. [Cited: January 1, 2025.] https://www.debt.org/faqs/americans-in-debt/demographics/.

16. **Eli, Gomez, [writ.].** *Extreme Couponing.* [prod.] Matt Sharp. Sharp Entertainment; TLC, 2010 - 2012.

17. **Cincinnati Family Magazine.** Teaching Kids to be Savvy Shoppers. *Cincinnati Family Magazine.* [Online] October 31, 2012. [Cited: January 3, 2025.] https://cincinnatifamilymagazine.com/teaching-kids-to-be-savvy-shoppers/.

18. **Gravier, Elizabeth.** The No. 1 money behavior kids learn from their parents. *CNBC.* [Online] May 20, 2024. [Cited: January 5, 2025.] https://www.cnbc.com/select/how-kids-learn-about-money/.

19. **T. ROWE PRICE.** The 14th annual T. Rowe Price Parents, Kids & Money Survey. *TRowePrice.* [Online] April 5, 2022. https://tinyurl.com/5n6fttyx.

20. *When couples fight about money, what do they fight about?* **Peetz, Johanna, Meloff, Zoe and Royle, Courtney.** 11, s.l. : Journal of Social and Personal Relationships, July 5, 2023, Journal of Social and Personal Relationships, Vol. 40, pp. 3723 - 3751. https://journals.sagepub.com/doi/pdf/10.1177/02654075231187897. 10.1177/02654075231187897.

21. **Langabeer, James.** How to navigate conflicts and create healthy financial relationships. *Psychology Today.* [Online] Psychology Today, December 7, 2022. https://tinyurl.com/bdwb3mxr.

22. **Statista Research Department.** Coupon use in the United States 2017-2020. *Statista.* [Online] December 7, 2024. [Cited: January 12, 2025.] https://www.statista.com/statistics/240237/coupon-use-in-the-united-states/.

23. **Chevalier, Stephanie.** Importance of discount & coupons in digital purchases in the U.S. 2018, by age group. *Statista.* [Online] May 4, 2022. [Cited: January 12, 2025.]

https://www.statista.com/statistics/824001/users-importance-discounts-coupons-digital-purchasing-decisions/.

24. —. U.S. coupon acquisition websites 2018. *Statista.* [Online] December 7, 2024. [Cited: January 12, 2021.] https://www.statista.com/statistics/533429/preferred-coupon-search-websites/.

25. **Dating Detective.** Impact of Money Issues on Relationships Across America. *The Dating Detective Blog.* [Online] June 20, 2024. [Cited: January 13, 2025.] https://dating-detective.blog/impact-of-money-issues-on-relationships-across/.

26. **Kiernan, John S.** Late-Payment Survey. *WalletHub.* [Online] February 26, 2022. [Cited: January 14, 2025.] https://wallethub.com/blog/late-payments-survey/58680.

27. **Maxwell, Tim.** How to reconcile your bank statements. *Experian.* [Online] February 28, 2024. [Cited: January 15, 2025.] https://www.experian.com/blogs/ask-experian/how-to-reconcile-your-bank-statements/.

28. **Capital One Shopping.** Impulse Buying Statistics (2024): Consumer Spending Habits. *Capital One Shopping.* [Online] November 12, 2024. [Cited: January 16, 2025.] https://capitaloneshopping.com/research/impulse-buying-statistics/.

29. **Hayes, Marianne.** What is emotional spending? *Experian.* [Online] January 18, 2023. [Cited: January 18, 2025.] https://www.experian.com/blogs/ask-experian/what-is-emotional-spending/.

30. **McMullen, Laura.** What is impulse buying? 5 ways to resist. *NerdWallet.* [Online] November 8, 2024. [Cited: January 17, 2025.] https://www.nerdwallet.com/article/finance/impulse-buying-definition.

31. **Black, Dr. Donald W.** *A review of Compulsive Buying Disorder.* s.l. : World psychiatry : Official journal of the World Psychiatric Association (WPA), 2007. pp. 14 - 18.

https://pmc.ncbi.nlm.nih.gov/articles/PMC1805733/pdf/wpa060014.pdf.

32. **Melore, Chris.** Quality matters: 63 percent admit buying cheaper version of products wound up being big mistake. *Study Finds.* [Online] October 15, 2022. [Cited: January 17, 2025.] https://studyfinds.org/quality-products-last-longer-than-cheaper/.

33. **Kopp, Carol M.** Perceived value: what it is and why it's important. *Investopedia.* [Online] July 26, 2020. [Cited: January 17, 2024.] https://www.investopedia.com/terms/p/perceived-value.asp.

34. *Consumer Perceptions of Price, Quality, and Value: A Means-End Model and Synthesis of evidence.* **Zeithaml, Valarie A.** 3, July 1, 1988, Journal of Marketing, Vol. 52. https://www.researchgate.net/publication/282671247_Consumer_Perceptions_of_Price_Quality_and_Value_A_Means-End_Model_and_Synthesis_of_Evidence. 10.1177/002224298805200302.

35. **Lisa, Andrew.** 44 percent pay off their full credit card balance, survey finds: Pros and cons of this strategy. *GOBankingRates.* [Online] October 18, 2021. [Cited: 18 2025, January.] https://www.gobankingrates.com/credit-cards/advice/44-pay-off-their-full-credit-card-balance-each-month-heres-why-they-shouldnt/?utm_campaign=1145963&utm_source=yahoo.com&utm_content=20&utm_medium=rss.

36. **Federal Trade Commission.** Credit Card Accountability Responsibility and Disclosure Act of 2009 (Credit CARD Act). *Federal Trade Commission.* [Online] April 3, 2024. [Cited: January 18, 2025.] https://uscode.house.gov/statutes/pl/111/24.pdf. https://www.ftc.gov/legal-library/browse/statutes/credit-card-accountability-responsibility-disclosure-act-2009-credit-card-act.

37. **Campbell, Jesse.** How to tell if you're using too much credit. *Money Management International.* [Online] October 29, 2023. [Cited: January 19, 2025.] https://www.moneymanagement.org/blog/too-much-credit.

38. **Soucy, Paul.** NerdWallet's guide to your first credit card. *NerdWallet.* [Online] July 20, 2023. [Cited: January 20, 2025.] https://www.nerdwallet.com/article/credit-cards/nerdwallet-guide-first-credit-card.

39. **Cui, Jasmine.** Middle-class homeowners are increasingly squeezed by housing costs. *NBC News.* [Online] October 14, 2024. [Cited: January 21, 2025.] https://www.nbcnews.com/data-graphics/middle-class-new-homeowners-cost-burdened-house-poor-rcna163853.

40. **Olya, Gabrielle.** How much money do Americans have in their bank accounts in 2024? *GOBankingRates.* [Online] June 2024. https://www.gobankingrates.com/banking/banks/how-much-money-do-americans-have-in-their-bank-accounts-in-2024/.

41. **Collinson, Catherine and Cho, Heidi.** *24th Annual Transamerica Retirement Survey of Workers | The multigenerational workforce: life, work, & retirement.* Transamerica Institute. s.l. : Transamerica Center for Retirement Studies.

42. **Rocheleau, Stacy.** Marital Waste: How it impacts divorce settlements. *Right Lawyers.* [Online] November 20, 2024. [Cited: January 22, 2025.] https://rightlawyers.com/what-is-marital-waste/.

43. *Love, Lies, and Money: Financial infidelity in romantic relationships.* **Garbinsky, Emily N., et al.** 1, October 29, 2019, Journal of Consumer Research, Vol. 47, pp. 1 - 24. https://academic.oup.com/jcr/article-pdf/47/1/1/33183807/ucz052.pdf. 10.1093/jcr/ucz052.

44. **Kelton, Katie.** Survey: 2 in 5 Americans in a relationship have kept a financial secret from their partner. *Bankrate.* [Online] January 27, 2025. [Cited: February 4, 2025.] https://www.bankrate.com/credit-cards/news/financial-infidelity-survey/#leads.

45. *Pooling finances and relationship satisfaction.* **Gladstone, Joe J, Garbinsky, Emily N and Mogilner, Cassie.** 6, March 14, 2022, Journal of Personality and Social Psychology, Vol. 123, pp. 1293-

1314. https://doi.org/10.1037/pspi0000388. 10.1037/pspi0000388.

46. *Common cents: bank account structure and couples' relationship dynamics.* **Olson, Jenny G, et al.** 4, March 14, 2023, Journal of Consumer Research, Vol. 50, pp. 704-721. https://doi.org/10.1093/jcr/ucad020. 10.1093/jcr/ucad020.

47. **Staples, Ana.** Bankrate. *43 percent of U.S. couples living together only have joint accounts: Here's what's wrong with this trend.* [Online] March 19, 2022. [Cited: January 25, 2025.] https://www.bankrate.com/credit-cards/news/us-joint-account-survey/.

48. **Parker, Kim.** Americans see men as the financial providers, even as women's contributions grow. *Pew Research Center.* [Online] April 14, 2024. [Cited: Januaary 27, 2025.] https://www.pewresearch.org/short-reads/2017/09/20/americans-see-men-as-the-financial-providers-even-as-womens-contributions-grow/.

49. *Relationships between gender role attitudes, role division, and perception of equity among heterosexual, gay and lesbian couples.* **Shechory, Mally and Ziv, Riva.** 9-10, May 18, 2007, Sex Roles, Vol. 56, pp. 629–638. https://doi.org/10.1007/s11199-007-9207-3.

50. **Chapman, Gary D.** *The 5 love Languages.* 1st edition. s.l. : Northfield Publishing, 2014. 978-0802411402.

51. **Stolba, Stefan Lembo.** Married consumers have higher credit scores and debt than single adults. *Experian.* [Online] February 24, 2020. [Cited: February 2, 2025.] https://www.experian.com/blogs/ask-experian/research/married-couples-have-higher-credit-scores-and-debt-than-single-adults/.

52. **Brown, Natalia.** What is financial infidelity? | Hiding debt from spouse. *National Debt Relief.* [Online] February 28, 2023. [Cited: February 3, 2025.] https://www.nationaldebtrelief.com/blog/debt-guide/marital-debt/impossible-hide-money-spouse/#:~:text=Previous

percent20studies percent20have percent20found percent20that,So percent2C percent20the percent20stakes percent20are percent20high..

53. **Experian.** Is the honeymoon already over for today's newlyweds? *Experian.* [Online] May 2, 2016. [Cited: February 3, 2025.] https://www.experianplc.com/newsroom/press-releases/2016/newlywed-survey-2016.

54. **Fidelity Investments.** 2024 Couples & Money Study. *TheNewsMarket.com.* [Online] 2024. [Cited: January 24, 2025.] https://preview.thenewsmarket.com/Previews/FINP/DocumentAssets/660835_v4.pdf.

55. **Genius.** Frank Sinatra – Love and Marriage. *Genius.* [Online] [Cited: February 7, 2025.] https://genius.com/Frank-sinatra-love-and-marriage-lyrics.

56. **Kelton, Katie K.** Living Paycheck to Paycheck statistics. *Bankrate.* [Online] August 14, 2024. https://www.bankrate.com/credit-cards/news/living-paycheck-to-paycheck-statistics/.

57. **Lieber, Ron.** *The opposite of spoiled: Raising kids who are grounded, generous, and smart about money.* s.l. : Harper Collins, 2015. ISBN- 0062247026.

58. **Edlynn PhD, Emily.** Should I talk to my kids about our family's money problems? *Parents.* [Online] March 29, 2024. [Cited: February 12, 2025.] https://www.parents.com/should-i-talk-about-money-problems-with-my-kids-6745858#:~:text=But percent20addressing percent20money percent20and percent20family,skills percent20for percent20future percent20self percent2Dsufficiency..

59. *Talk is cheap: Parent financial socialization and emerging adult financial well-being.* **LeBaron-Black, Ashley B., et al.** 3, August 9, 2022, Family Relations, Vol. 72, pp. 1201-1219. https://doi.org/10.1111/fare.12751. 10.1111/fare.12751.

60. **Discover Student Loans.** Discover Student Loans Survey Finds More Parents Expect Their Child to Help Pay for College. *Discover*

Student LOans. [Online] July 29, 2019. [Cited: September 15, 2023.] https://www.businesswire.com/news/home/20190729005121/en/.

61. **Wood, Sarah.** See the Average College Tuition in 2024-2025. *US News & World Report.* [Online] September 26, 2024. [Cited: February 15, 2025.] https://www.usnews.com/education/best-colleges/paying-for-college/articles/paying-for-college-infographic.

INDEX

5

A

B

C

D

R

S

T

U

V

W

Z

www.ingramcontent.com/pod-product-compliance
Lightning Source LLC
LaVergne TN
LVHW070832220926
848486LV00035B/421/J